THE OREGON EXPERIMENT

The Oregon Experiment is the third in a series of books which describe an entirely new attitude to architecture and planning. The books are intended to provide a complete working alternative to our present ideas about architecture, building, and planning—an alternative which will, we hope, gradually replace current ideas and practices.

Center for Environmental Structure
BERKELEY, CALIFORNIA

THE
OREGON
EXPERIMENT

Christopher Alexander
Murray Silverstein
Shlomo Angel
Sara Ishikawa
Denny Abrams

NEW YORK

OXFORD UNIVERSITY PRESS

1975

9   10

Printed in the United States of America
on acid-free paper

An instant in the process

We expected . . . the usual architect-user relation: we would pour out our problems . . . and we expected the planners to come back with a picture. But it kept coming back to us . . . they kept drawing it out of us. . . . We went out in the mud, in the rain, and looked at the site . . . tried to imagine places . . . how should the main entrance be located, what is it like . . . we looked at the imaginary places. . . . What did we envision as happening there? Slowly, little by little, we started seeing it . . . the pieces started to fit together. . . . It seemed the planners were there to draw it out of us; to make us come to grips with the problems. It was a very exciting week.

Later on, different groups contributed to the work. The secretaries drew up an office plan for the administration. Each one made a drawing . . . then they picked the best. . . . The financial secretary came up with it. . . . She said, "This is how we want it. . . ." And so we put it in. . . .

John McManus

Professor of Music,
University of Oregon,
speaking to architects, AIA Convention Workshop,
May 1973, San Francisco

CONTENTS

THE OREGON EXPERIMENT

INTRODUCTION

This book is the master plan for the University of Oregon. It also defines a process which can, with minor modifications, be adopted as a master plan by any community, anywhere in the world. And it is also the third in a series of books which describes an entirely new attitude to architecture and planning—the first one of the series which explains in full practical detail how these ideas may be implemented. It is in this sense that the book describes an experiment. If the experiment takes hold, we hope that it will be a paradigm for projects in similar communities all over the world.

The University of Oregon has about 15,000 students and 3300 faculty and staff (1973). It occupies a site on the outskirts of Eugene, a small town with about 84,000 inhabitants. The university was founded in the mid-nineteenth century. For most of its life it has had a few thousand students; only during the last 10 years have there been more than 10,000 students. The very rapid growth of the last few years created a crisis, fairly typical of fast growing communities, besieged by multi-million dollar buildings, built with government funds, especially in the technological fields. The University, swamped by these technocratic invasions, in peril of its life, needed a master plan to control its growth, and make the campus environment reasonable, alive, and healthy once again— as it had been during the early years of its growth. We persuaded the university authorities that this could only be done if they were willing to entertain an entirely new kind of planning process. They agreed to try this process.

The process itself is one practical manifestation of the theoretical ideas presented in Volumes 1 and 2.

Volume 1, *The Timeless Way of Building*, describes a theory of planning and building which is, essentially, a modern post-industrial version of the age-old pre-industrial and traditional processes which shaped the world's most beautiful towns and buildings for thousands of years.

Volume 2, *A Pattern Language*, is an explicit set of instructions for designing and building, which defines patterns at every scale, from the structure of a region to the nailing of a window; set out in such a way that laymen can use it to design a satisfying and ecologically appropriate environment for themselves and their activities.

Volume 3, this book, is the master plan for the University of Oregon, and describes a practical way of implementing these ideas in a community. However, we must emphasize at once that we are dealing here with a very special kind of community. Unlike most communities, it has a single owner (The State of Oregon), and a single, centralized budget. This situation is not only unusual, it is even opposite to the ideas which are actually needed to make the way of building which we call the timeless way, appear in a society. However, we believe that a modified version of this way of building is possible, even under these restrictions, and this book, beyond its function as a master plan for the University of Oregon, is our attempt to define this process.

The process will apply, in full, to any other community where there is a single owner, and a single centralized budget. This means that it will apply, for example, to a kibbutz, a hospital, a corporate industrial plant, a farm, a cooperative factory, any settlement where the concept of private property has been abolished, and any benevolent institution run by a government for the welfare of its citizens.

We repeat, that we do not consider these kinds of institutions ideal. In a future book we shall describe the process of implementation that is needed in a more ideal neighborhood or community, where people own their houses, common land and workshops, and where there is no centralized budget. In this book, we nevertheless propose a process which can allow people under the half-ideal conditions of the centralized budget, to take care of the environment for themselves, and have some measure of control over their own lives.

Throughout this book we are especially concerned with the practical steps which must be taken to make these things happen. Specifically, we believe that the process of building and planning in a community will create an environment which meets human needs only if it follows six principles of implementation:

1. The principle of organic order.
2. The principle of participation.
3. The principle of piecemeal growth.
4. The principle of patterns.
5. The principle of diagnosis.
6. The principle of coordination.

We recommend that the University of Oregon, and any other institution or community which has a single owner, and a centralized budget, adopt these six principles to replace its conventional master planning and conventional budgetary procedures, to provide the administrative resources which will guarantee people the right to design their own places, and to set in motion the democratic processes which will ensure their flexible continuation.

For the sake of concreteness, and to give you an overview of the book, we now outline these six principles.

1. The principle of organic order.
Planning and construction will be guided by a process which allows the whole to emerge gradually from local acts.

2. The principle of participation.
All decisions about what to build, and how to build it, will be in the hands of the users.

3. The principle of piecemeal growth.
The construction undertaken in each budgetary period will be weighed overwhelmingly towards small projects.

4. The principle of patterns.

All design and construction will be guided by a collection of communally adopted planning principles called patterns.

5. The principle of diagnosis.

The well being of the whole will be protected by an annual diagnosis which explains, in detail, which spaces are alive and which ones dead, at any given moment in the history of the community.

6. The principle of coordination.

Finally, the slow emergence of organic order in the whole will be assured by a funding process which regulates the stream of individual projects put forward by users.

In the six chapters which follow, these principles are defined in much greater detail. You may, if you like, treat each chapter as an argument which culminates in the detailed presentation of one of these principles. Within each chapter, the principles are discussed—as they were derived—in the context of our work as master planners for the University of Oregon. Our examples are drawn from the University of Oregon, and many of our implementary procedures are written to be consistent with present conditions at the University of Oregon. We did consider trying to write in more general terms—but we decided finally that as a book on practice it is more clear, and more convincing, because it is so firmly anchored in the specific details of the University of Oregon.

Anyone who reads what we have written about these principles will be able to modify them to suit his own community. And finally, although these principles are written to apply to communities with one owner and a centralized budget, we believe that modified, decentralized, versions of these principles will probably have to be followed in all communities where people seek comparably human and organic results. In this sense, then, we believe that the cores of these six principles are fundamental to all processes in which the timeless way of building can arise in our society.

The University of Cambridge

CHAPTER I

ORGANIC ORDER

In the middle twentieth century, most communities which try to take a responsible attitude to their environments have adopted, or intend to adopt, an instrument of planning policy called a "master plan," to control the individual acts of building which go on there. In different countries this master plan is also called a general plan, a development plan, an outline plan.

Master plans take many forms; but almost all of them have one thing in common. They include a map, which specifies the future growth of the community, and prescribes the land uses, functions, heights, and other qualities which may, or should, be built in different areas.

These maps, and master plans, are intended to coordinate the many hundreds of otherwise independent acts of building. They are intended to make sure, in a word, that the many acts of building in a community will together gradually help to create a whole, instead of merely making up an aggregation of unrelated parts, a chaos.

In this first chapter we shall argue that the master plan, as currently conceived, cannot create a whole. It can create a totality, but not a whole. It can create totalitarian order, but not organic order. We shall argue, in short, that although the task of making sure that individual acts of building cooperate to form a whole is real, the conventional master plan—based on a map of the future—cannot possibly perform this task. As we shall see, the conventional master plan cannot solve the basic problem, because it is too rigid to do so—and, because, in addition, it creates an entirely new set of other problems, more devastating in human terms than the chaos it is meant to govern.

In presenting this argument, we shall restate, in some degree, the arguments already presented in *The Timeless Way of Building:* but we shall now focus on the practical questions which are created by these arguments.

Let us begin with the idea of organic order. Everyone is aware that most of the built environment today lacks a natural order, an order which presents itself very strongly in places that were built centuries ago. This natural or organic order emerges when there is perfect balance between the needs of the individual parts of the environment, and the needs of the whole. In an organic environment, every place is unique, and the different places also cooperate, with no parts left over, to create a global whole—a whole which can be identified by everyone who is a part of it.

The University of Cambridge is a perfect example of organic order. One of the most beautiful features of this university is the way that the colleges—St. Johns, Trinity, Trinity Hall, Clare, Kings, Peterhouse, Queens—lie between the main street of the town and the river. Each college is a system of residential courts, each college has its entrance on the street, and opens onto the river; each college has its own small bridge that crosses the river, and leads to the meadows beyond; each college has its own boathouse and its own walks along the river. But while each college repeats the same system, each one has its own unique character. The individual courts, entrances, bridges, boathouses, and walks are all different. The overall organization of all the colleges together and the individual characteristics of each college is perhaps the most wonderful thing about Cambridge. It is a perfect example of organic order. At each level there is a perfect balance and harmony of parts.

Where did this order come from? Of course it was not planned; there was no master plan. And yet, the regularity, the order, is far too profound to have happened purely by chance. Somehow, the combination of tacit, culture-defined agreements, and traditional approaches to well-known problems, insured that even when people were working separately, they were still working together, sharing the same principles. As a result, no matter how unique and individual the pieces were, there was always underlying order in the whole.

Today, this is a lost art. Nowadays, the process of growth and development almost never seems to manage to create this subtle balance between the importance of the individual parts, and the coherence of the environment as a whole. One or the other always dominates.

In some cases the parts take control, and the whole is lost. This has happened, for example, at the University of California at Berkeley. A campus that was once beautiful, is now a litter of fragmented buildings, each one different, each one occupied with its own local problems. The many buildings do not form a whole together. There is functional breakdown at the level of the campus as a whole: the streets are congested; circulation is a maze.

Berkeley: The parts are more important than the whole

In other cases the whole is made to take control, and the integrity of the parts is lost. This has happened, for example, at the Chicago Circle campus of the University of Illinois. The university has been conceived as a totality by a group of architects; and the needs of individual places, or individual groups, are entirely submerged in the totalitarian order imposed by the architectural concept. There is a functional breakdown in the rooms within the buildings: they are arbitrarily shaped, without windows, etc. There is a kind of order in the whole, but no possibility of order in the parts.

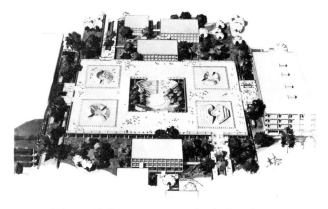

Chicago Circle: The whole straightjackets the parts

We define organic order as the kind of order that is achieved when there is a perfect balance between the needs of the parts, and the needs of the whole.

The University of Cambridge is a wonderful place, because it is an organic environment in just this sense. Today, however, the process by which the University of Cambridge was created no longer holds. Traditions have vanished; problems change fast; cultural agreements have disappeared; individual acts of building carried out within tradition, can no longer be relied upon to create organic order. In desperation, people who are concerned with the environment have come to believe that the environment must be planned—for many years in advance—to achieve the kind of order which came into being so naturally in earlier times.

And it is certainly true that nowadays communities do need a plan, or planning process of some kind. Without a plan, the gradual accumulation of piecemeal acts will create a thousand mistakes of organization, twisted relationships and missed opportunities. Without a plan for the University of Oregon, what guarantees have we that the road system which emerges will in the end be simple and easy to follow? How can we be sure that the distribution of parking meets the current needs? How can we be sure that the Willamette riverfront and its potential beauty will not gradually be destroyed by random development? And how can we be sure that as departments grow, they create a fabric of common interest and function, and not a chaos of random extensions?

In short, unplanned growth can easily lead to a loss of coordination between parts, and chaos in the whole. In today's fragmented scene we can no longer rely on unplanned piecemeal construction to create organic order. Without a planning process of some kind, there is not a chance in the world that the University of Oregon will ever come to possess an order anywhere near as deep and harmonious as the order that underlies the University of Cambridge.

The master plan has been the conventional way of approaching this difficulty. The master plan attempts to set down enough guidelines to provide for coherence in the environment as a whole—and still leave freedom for individual buildings and open spaces to adapt to local needs. Nearly every large campus has adopted some form of master plan; over the years the University of Oregon has had several.

Let us examine the idea in some detail. Essentially a university master plan is a map. It is a map which portrays the university as it "ought" to be, at some fairly distant future time—say twenty years from now. The map contains two kinds of elements—those which exist already and should, according to the planners, stay where they are; and those which do not now exist, and which need to be built. Since this map presents a picture of the future university as a whole, it is fairly easy to make sure that on the map, housing, teaching, roads, parking, open space, are all related to one another in a coherent manner.

☐ existing buildings
☐ new buildings

A conventional master plan, University of Oregon, 1961

Implementing such a plan, at least according to theory, is simply a matter of filling in the blanks, according to the land uses prescribed by the map. If the process is carried out faithfully, then the built university, after the prescribed number of years, will correspond to the ideal map of the master plan; and all the various parts of this future university will form a coherent whole, because they are simply plugged into the slots of the design.

This approach seems sensible in theory. But in practice master plans fail—because they create totalitarian order, not organic order. They are too rigid; they cannot easily adapt to the natural and unpredictable changes that inevitably arise in the life of a community. As these changes occur—in community sentiment, politics, opportunity—the master plan becomes obsolete, and is no longer followed. And even to the extent that master plans *are* followed, they do nothing to ensure for each building, a sound, human relationship to all the places around it. They do not specify enough about connections between buildings, human scale, balanced function, etc., to help each local act of building and design become well-related to the environment as a whole.

In effect, these two failures are two sides of the same coin: *It is simply not possible to fix today what the environment should be like twenty years from today, and then to steer the piecemeal process of development toward that fixed, imaginary world.*

Only totalitarian fantasy even makes it seem that such a course is possible. The attempt to steer such a course is rather like filling in the colors in a child's coloring book, where an outline figure has been drawn and the child then colors in the various parts according to the numbers written there. At best, the order which results from such a process is banal.

Let us illustrate these problems with two examples from the Eugene campus. First, the problem of rigidity. In 1961 the University of Oregon adopted a master plan. Among other things, this plan showed the destruction of the beautiful old pioneer cemetery to the south of campus, and showed future buildings built on the land where the cemetery had been. A "save the cemetery" group sprang up, and its efforts were successful. The university agreed to preserve the cemetery as a historical landmark. But as a result, the entire master plan which showed construction in the cemetery was shaken. The scale and density of buildings planned for the area around the cemetery were meant to relate to the built-up cemetery. The layout of the entire southwest quadrant of the university, including a proposed behavioral science complex, had been planned according to its relationships to the built-up cemetery. Once it became clear that the university no longer intended to build in the cemetery, these relationships became dubious. The whole area needed to be replanned. The buildings intended for the cemetery needed another slot in the plan; perhaps the density of the campus as a whole needed to change. To correct for these changes properly, it would have been necessary to draw an entirely new master plan. But of course a new plan was not drawn. There was neither money nor energy to do it. As for the plans which remained—clearly it was too rigid. It could not adapt in a fluent way to changing realities in the community. In this way, every master plan becomes less and less real, until people finally ignore it altogether because it no longer tells them anything useful.

Now let us take the case where the master plan *is* followed. The three dormitories on the east side of the campus were planned and sited according to an Area Master Plan, created in 1962, as part of an urban renewal project.

The plan shows the siting of dormitories on the east side of the campus. The map appears to be well-ordered; and, indeed, the dormitories have been built more or less according to this plan. But

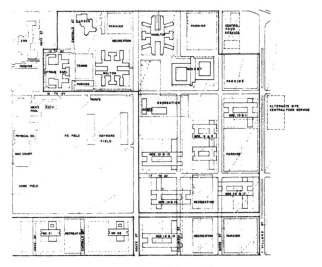

*Housing Area Master Plan—this map seems
sensible and harmless. . . .*

visiting these dormitories today, one is struck by
the grossness and arbitrariness of their geometry.
One is in the form of a pinwheel; another is a
kind of double cross; still another is shaped
around enclosed courtyards. But they lack all the
subtleties of detail which are needed to make them
comfortable and human.

The fundamental relationships that must be
maintained between buildings and the open space
around them, if the places are to be humanly com-

. . . but when the buildings are actually built,
they are not well adapted to their surroundings

fortable are missing: and the master plan does
nothing to infuse its parts, these buildings, with
these relationships. The master plan seems to suggest that the buildings which fill in the slots can
have any shape at all. It does not specify the critical relationships which buildings must have in
common, to make them functioning members of

the same family. And of course, it can't. If the buildings were drawn in any more detail on the master plan, to guide these subtler local relationships, the plan would not be flexible enough when it came time to build the individual buildings.

Thus, as a source of organic order, a master plan is both too precise, and not precise enough. The totality is too precise: the details are not precise enough. It fails because each part hinges on a conception of a "totality," which cannot respond to the inevitable accidents of time and still maintain its order. And it fails because as a result of its rigidity, it cannot afford to guide the details around buildings which really matter; if drawn in detail, these details would be absurdly rigid.

Master plans have two additional unhealthy characteristics. To begin with, the existence of a master plan alienates the users—in this case the students, faculty, and staff. After all, the very existence of a master plan means, by definition, that the members of the community can have little impact on the future shape of their community, because most of the important decisions have already been made. In a sense, under a master plan people are living with a frozen future, able to affect only relatively trivial details. When people

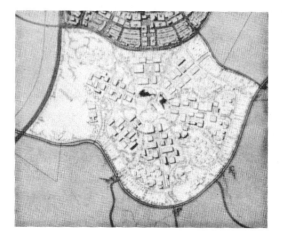

The University of California, Irvine Campus.
Can the people of the community identify
with this master plan?

lose the sense of responsibility for the environment they live in, and realize that they are merely cogs in someone else's machine, how can they feel any sense of identification with the community, or any sense of purpose there?

Second, neither the users nor the key decision makers can visualize the actual implications of the master plan. For example, a master plan was recently adopted by the town of Gothenberg, Sweden. After its adoption, sociologists interviewed the various legislators who had voted for it. It turned out that most of these men simply did not understand the plan; in some cases they could not even read the map of the plan correctly.

If people cannot even understand the concrete and human implications of a master plan after studying it, then it is extremely dangerous and foolish to rely on such a plan as a guide to future

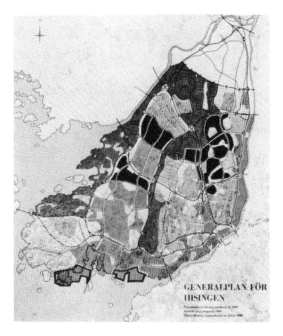

GENERALPLAN FÖR HISINGEN

A typical master plan. Can you understand what is going on here?

development. Whatever tool is used to guide development must be a tool which people can understand in concrete and human terms, and in terms of their everyday experience.

In summary then, we cannot recommend the conventional master plan for the University of Oregon, nor for any other community. We do not believe the master plan can succeed in coordinating acts of building, over the years, in a way that brings organic order to the whole. And we believe that a conventional master plan will have dangerous side effects on the community—it will sustain the rift that has grown up between users and their environment.

The first steps that have to be taken, to improve this situation, are expressed by the following principle.

The principle of organic order: Planning and construction will be guided by a process which allows the whole to emerge gradually from local acts. To this end, the community shall not adopt any form of physical master plan, but shall instead adopt the process which this book describes; the most basic fact of this process is that it enables the community to draw its order, not from a fixed map of the future, but from a communal pattern language; the process shall be administered, on behalf of the community, by a single planning board of less than 10 members, made up of users and administrators in about equal numbers, and a director of planning; the director of planning shall have a staff, of roughly one person/2000 population, to guide community action.

This principle is made more precise by the following details:

(i) *The community shall not adopt any form of physical master plan, but shall instead adopt the process which this book describes.*

The master plan idea was a serious attempt to infuse the environment with order. Eliminating the plan is not a call for chaos. Rather it is an attempt to overcome the difficulties inherent in this way of ordering the environment: the impossibility of making accurate predictions about future needs and resources; the ignorance of the more minute relationships between places which are not prescribed in the plan; the insensitivity of the plan to the ongoing needs of users; and the alienating quality of the plan as an administrative device.

We wish to replace this way of ordering the

environment with a growth process: a process so well defined that a community can adopt it, point by point; a process which does not rely for order on a prearranged map of the future, but instead stimulates thousands of local projects, aimed directly at meeting immediate, felt, needs.

The principles detailed in this book define such a process. There are six major principles, each with its associated subprinciples. The subprinciples can either be adopted exactly as they stand, or in some modified form which suits local circumstances. This means that the process as a whole can be formally adopted, not only by the University of Oregon, but also in modified form by any other similar community.

(ii) *The most basic fact of this process is that it enables the community to draw its order, not from a fixed map of the future, but from a communal pattern language.*

This fact, the cornerstone of everything that follows, is presented completely in the first two volumes of this series, *The Timeless Way of Building* and *A Pattern Language.*

In Chapter 4 we shall explain how the present process can be connected with the published pattern language. For the moment, we simply wish to make it clear that our call for a *process*, instead of a physical master plan, is not a pious hope based merely on the shortcomings of the physical master plan. The fact is that we are in a position to replace the master plan with a process, because the tools and theory needed for this process have already been worked out.

(iii) *The process shall be administered, on behalf of the community, by a single planning board of less than ten members, made up of users and administrators in about equal numbers, and a director of planning.*

The same damage that can be done to the community by a preconceived master plan can also be done by a centralized power group initiating and executing projects. The master plan cannot create organic order because it is insensitive to the subtle variety of forces which are inherent in different parts of the community. The same problem arises when a small group of individuals has too much power or control over the initiation and execution of projects in the community.

An administrator who has to make a large number of decisions about the very complex questions which arise in a community, cannot afford the time to go deeply into each of the questions which arises.

He must inevitably make his decisions, then, on the basis of an undifferentiated, unsubtle view of the forces at work. This will happen no matter how far sighted, or how well disposed he is. It is inevitable, therefore, that he will make decisions largely influenced by his own "opinions," his own idiosyncracies—and not by the thousands, and tens of thousands of actual forces at work in the real situation.

Under these circumstances, the buildings which are built will inevitably reflect these idiosyncratic opinions, and will, like buildings based on a master plan, be improperly adapted to the myriad of subtle influences which are at work in a lively community.

In order to correct these natural defects which will occur in any system where power is too centralized, it is essential, first and foremost, that all projects be initiated by their users—not by the administration. This is discussed fully in Chapter 2. But even when centralized decision-making power is offset by a process in which projects are initiated by the users, the vital question of administration and steering still remains. The multitude of individual projects which emerge from a large community must still be coordinated by some kind of executive action. What form should this executive action take, to maintain the balance of organic growth?

At present, this steering process is handled at the University of Oregon by three different groups: a very small group of top level administrators, who help the president make the final decisions about budgets and programs; a committee of eighteen users, called the campus planning committee, which advises the president's top administrators; and an entirely separate campus planning staff, which reports to the top administrators, and also acts as staff for the campus planning committee.

Of these three groups, the campus planning committee has played the central role. If any one of the three is responsible for "the planning process" today, it is this committee. However, we believe that the present threefold division of responsibility is working against the needs of an organic planning process: and we propose to strengthen the campus planning committee by making it into a single executive planning board which brings together the strengths of all three groups, in balance, and allows them, together, to take complete responsibility for administering and steering the planning process.

The great strength of the campus planning committee has been its emphasis on users. It has nine students, five faculty, and four administrators —and is thus heavily weighted toward the users. The great importance of the users is not that they represent the people of the university in any official political sense, but rather that they speak for themselves, as ordinary persons, who can base their observations and decisions on their everyday experience; they are not forced, by their position, to base their decisions on abstract considerations about programs and money.

However, the present campus planning committee is weighted so heavily toward the users, that it has almost no serious working relationship with the administrators. It is true that four top level administrators have ex-officio seats on the committee—but this is more a matter of courtesy than anything else.

The administrators are so heavily outnumbered, that they cannot possibly contemplate executive action while sitting on the committee. Instead, they see their presence on the committee as a matter of liaison and information only; they are virtually forced, by the nature of the situation, to make their key decisions in private—away from the deliberations of the committee. And no one can blame them. From the standpoint of the administrators, the committee is too unwieldy for serious decision-making.

This drastically reduces the effectiveness of the committee. Decisions are made without reference to the most weighty matters which the administrators are trying to account for; and as a result the recommendations made by the committee cannot possibly be treated as anything more than information by the administrators.

Obviously, it would be far better if the user-oriented function of the committee could be combined with the executive power of the top level administrators. Then there is some chance that balanced decisions could be hammered out and implemented. But this will only happen if the board has about equal numbers of users and administrators; and if it is small enough to make decision-making practical.

In this sense, the present campus planning committee is far too large. Difficult points cannot be discussed seriously, because the discussions become too diffuse—any committee with eighteen people on it, meeting only a few hours a month, cannot hope to do anything but ramble. We propose that the planning board have seven, or at the most nine members. Common human experience suggests that seven is about the upper limit to the number of people who can make decisions together, without delegating decisions to a subcommittee. And we believe it should be constituted as a "board," not a "committee," a group able to take far greater responsibility than the present committee.

We believe also that the director of planning should be part of the planning board. He will often know more about the process than any other single person; and, most important, since he, or someone from his staff, will be in direct touch with user groups, he will be in an excellent position to explain the user's case—to argue its strengths and weaknesses. We suggest, however, to avoid any possible conflict of interest, that while the director of planning sit on the board, he not be a voting member.

To embody all these features, we suggest that the planning board might be a seven member board, including two students, two faculty members, one of them drawn from the administration, two top level administrators, and the director of planning.

(iv) *The director of planning shall have a staff, of roughly one person/2000 population, to guide community action.*

The planning board can administer the process. But they cannot possibly take care of the day to day work which the process requires—especially since, as we shall see, the process requires that the initiation of projects be entirely decentralized and put into the hands of local groups. To help this along the director of planning needs a staff. And it is crucial that this staff be large enough. The University of Oregon planning staff has, in the last three years, been cut from three and one-half to two and one-half to two full time positions. With such a small staff it has been almost impossible for the process to work effectively.

We estimate that the Eugene campus, a community of about 20,000 persons, will generate at least 60 projects per year, when the process is working effectively. Experience with the pattern language, and with user groups, suggests that any one person can handle about six new projects per year, together with the work of carrying old projects forward. At this rate, a community which generates 60 new projects per year would need a full time staff of 10. We do not expect that the University can support a full time paid professional staff of 10. However, we do believe that they can approach this figure. First, half of the 10 at least can be para-professionals—lay persons, or trainees, with enough skill to help perform the functions of this process. In Oregon, architecture and planning students can function in this manner; lay people who have experienced the process themselves, can also serve to help others. Secondly, as we shall see, since this process replaces the schematic design phase of architectural projects, some of the money normally set aside for professional architects could be redirected to increase the staff.

The staff should include planners, architects, builders, and other professionals with knowledge of maintenance, community planning problems, etc. Any other similar professionals who are part of the community—at Oregon, the campus architect, and the director of physical plant—should also be members of this staff, their work coordinated by the planning director. The common bond between these different members of the staff should not be any presently known professional discipline. It should simply be that all the members of the staff understand, and have a working knowledge of the planning process which this book describes; and above all that they are people who feel at home working *with* user groups—people who will not take over the reins of design jobs and impose an arbitrary order on them. We suggest that the first book in this series, *The Timeless Way of Building,* be treated as a manual for the staff. It will help maintain the mood that is proper to straightforward, indigenous design.

CHAPTER 2

Only the people can guide the process of organic growth in a community. They know the most about their own needs, and they know most about how well or how badly the rooms and buildings, paths and open spaces are working. We start, therefore, with the people who live and work in the University of Oregon at Eugene—the students, faculty and staff.

No matter how well architects and planners plan, or how carefully they design, they cannot by themselves create environments that have the variety and the order we are after. An organic mixture can only be made by the action of a community, in which everyone helps to shape the parts of the environment that he knows best.

The arguments for this are presented in full detail in *The Timeless Way of Building*. We shall summarize those arguments here; but what we are concerned with, above all, in this book are the practicalities involved. Can it be done? Do the faculty and students have enough time available to them to take part? Are the practical arrangements with architects of such a kind that the users are actually able to express their ideas, without having them ridiculed and distorted? Is the information in the pattern language actually powerful enough to let people make designs for themselves? Are the building projects small enough to make this process practically feasible? Do people have enough stake in a community which they do not actually own to make responsible decisions? To what extent do the users need guidance, and where do they get it from while they are designing with the pattern language?

Let us begin by asking exactly what "participation" means. It can mean any process by which the users of an environment help to shape it. The most modest kind of participation is the kind where the user helps to shape a building by acting as a client for an architect. The fullest kind of participation is the kind where users actually build their buildings for themselves.

For the Eugene campus we advocate an intermediate kind of participation, in which the buildings are designed by the users and are then built by architects and contractors. In this process schematic designs are prepared by groups of faculty, students, and staff. Architects then help to implement the users' designs; but the essence of the design is created by the users.

Let us try to explain why we believe this form of participation is so important for the University.

There are essentially two reasons. First, participation is inherently good; it brings people together, involves them in their world; it creates feeling between people and the world around them, because it is a world which *they* have helped to make. Second, the daily users of buildings know more about their needs than anyone else; so the process of participation tends to create places which are better adapted to human functions than those created by a centrally administered planning process.

Let us begin with the idea of participation as an intrinsic good. When we say that people are more able to become involved in the world they live in when they take part in its design, there are actually two aspects to this thought. On the one hand, people need the chance to make active decisions about the environment. This is a fundamental human need. It is a need to create; and a need for control. Whenever people have the opportunity to change the environment around them, they do it, they enjoy it, and they gain enormous satisfaction from what they have done. On the other hand, people need a chance to identify with the part of the environment in which they live and work; they want some sense of ownership, some sense of territory. The most vital question about the various places in any community is always this: Do the people who use them own them psychologically? Do they feel that they can do with them as they they wish; do they feel that the place is theirs; are they free to make the place their own?

These two aspects of involvement—creative control and ownership—are of course related. You cannot control a place unless to some extent you own it. And you cannot have a sense of ownership unless to some extent you can control it. Students and faculty will never feel any true sense of involvement in the university unless to some extent they own their labs and offices, and unless, to some extent, they can control the changes there to suit themselves. The first reason to encourage participation, then, is that it allows people to become involved in their community, because it

Part of Goddard College, Vermont, designed and built by the students and faculty · · ·

gives them some sense of ownership, and some degree of control.

We come now to the second reason for participation: the fact that the users of a building know more about their needs than anyone else; the fact

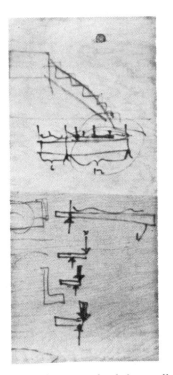

. . . drawings were sketched on walls
as work progressed

that it is virtually impossible to get a building which is well adapted to these needs if the people who are the actual users do not design it.

At the university, there are countless stories of frustrated scientists trying to describe the nature

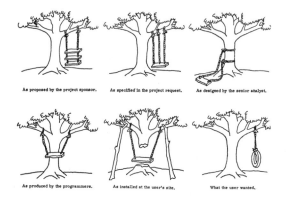

As proposed by the project sponsor.   As specified in the project request.   As designed by the senior analyst.

As produced by the programmers.   As installed at the user's site.   What the user wanted.

of a laboratory to an architect. The scientists always seem unable to communicate their needs to the architect. They end up with buildings that have too little light, too little acoustic isolation in the crucial places, not enough storage, no places to sit and think, no windows where they are needed, on and on. It happens all the time. We heard several versions of this story from students and faculty who work in the new science buildings at the University of Oregon.

To some degree this difficulty can be overcome by the use of patterns from *A Pattern Language*. The patterns define qualities a building must have to meet human needs. But there are countless needs and subtleties that are not defined by these patterns. When a man designs an office for himself, he takes these extra, subtle needs into account as a matter of course, because he can feel them. But when he has to explain these needs to an architect, the only ones which get across are the ones which he can state in words.

It is clear then, that participation has important advantages. There are, however, two important objections to the idea of participation. First: "Participation will create chaos, because in design and planning, people don't know what they are doing." Second: "Most students, and many faculty, stay at the university for less than five years; there is, therefore, no reason why they should design the places in the university since, after five years, the actual users will no longer be the same people as the users who made the designs."

We first discuss the objection that user-design will create chaos. The recent history of architecture and planning has created the false impression that architects and planners are the only people who know how to lay out buildings. The evidence from the last two or three thousand years of human history tells the opposite story. Almost all the environments in human history have been designed by lay people. Many of the most wonderful places in the world, now avidly photographed by architects, were not designed by architects but by lay people.

Architecture by the people: a town in Switzerland

But of course, in order to create order, not chaos, people must have some shared principles. Nothing would be worse than an environment in which each square foot was designed according to entirely different principles. This would be chaos indeed. In our proposal, this problem is solved by the use of the shared "patterns" which we present in Chapter 4. These patterns give the users a solid base for their design decisions. Each person and group of people will be able to make unique places, but always within the morphological framework created by the patterns. In short, the patterns play the role, within the university, that tradition played in a traditional culture. Within a framework of shared patterns, we can be sure that the process of participation will create a rich and various order.

The objection that participation does not make sense, because the users who design the university today will not be users in the years to come, is more subtle. At first sight it seems correct. But it is incorrect, in fact, because it is based on a misunderstanding of the real purpose and effect of user design.

When a group of Ph.D. students design a coffee lounge where they can discuss physics, the place which they create is not adapted primarily to their needs as Tom and George and Mary. First and foremost, the lounge is adapted to the needs of a group of Ph.D. students discussing physics, and as such it should be as comfortable for the next group of Ph.D. students as for the group which designed it. Of course it will not match the needs of any later group of users perfectly. But before you over-emphasize this difficulty, remember the alternative. The alternative is that the design is not made by users *at all*, but by a group of architects and administrators who are still more remote from the users' needs.

In other words, there is no way of avoiding the fact that university buildings will be designed by people different from the ones who end up using it in later years. The only question is: How different shall they be? It seems clear that we should choose people who are as similar as possible in their needs and habits as the people who will ultimately use the building. Since one group of Ph.D. students knows more about the needs of another group of Ph.D. students than any group of architects and administrators can possibly know, it seems clear that we should put the design in the hands of the users, even though we know they will be followed by generations of other users and are not designing the building only for themselves.

To drive the point home: on the housing market, personal and individual houses are always worth more than mass-produced houses. When you buy such a house, it fits you better, *not* because you are the person who created it, but simply because a *particular person* created it. This simple fact in itself is enough to guarantee that the places in the house are more real, better adapted to use, and more closely in tune with the actuality of living, than any house created impersonally for the mass market, by a designer.

The same can happen in the university. As places are created and modified by the people who pass through them, the university will gradually be shaped by an accumulation of actual human experience and, as such, will be a place fit for other, newer human experiences—a place far fitter than any impersonal and inflexible environment could ever be.

It is clear, from all this, that participation is desirable. But is it actually possible? Is the kind of participation we advocate attainable, under modern social conditions? Can a design conceived directly by lay people have the qualities of life and order that good architects give to their buildings?

To answer these questions, we now present a building project designed by a group of faculty and staff and students at the University of Oregon. The project is a design for a rather large part of a building: a half-million dollar extension to the music school and substantial repair of the existing building. The project is based on a design procedure that will be explained in detail in Chapter

49

6. We present it now to show immediately that participation can in fact succeed.

Project for the School of Music. The present Music School is cramped and partly derelict. The practice rooms are not well insulated; there are few places where faculty and students can meet informally; the building's entrances are not clearly marked; there is no place for small public recitals; the noise from passing traffic disturbs people working in the studios. Earlier analysis suggested that some 16,000 square feet of new building would be needed to solve these problems. At our suggestion, the dean of music agreed that he and a group of people from the department, would themselves make a design for the new space, according to the process which we have proposed. A group of seven was chosen: the Dean, three members of the faculty, a student, and two of us. We seven formed the core group. We worked together for one full week, developing a schematic design. During the week other persons were brought into the group, as matters concerning them arose. The university planner helped in the discussion of pedestrian movement; the instrument repair man was invited to design and locate his workshop; undergraduates were asked to conceive of a plan for safe, private storage of their instruments.

The work started with a survey of the existing buildings. The survey showed which parts of the existing buildings could be left intact because they were working well; which parts required repair; and which parts needed a complete overhaul. The dean and faculty added a program which described the various kinds of new spaces which were needed.

Then the group set about the design. Design decisions were made step by step, taking one pattern at a time, in the manner we describe in Chapter 6, page 170. The patterns used to generate the drawings are presented in Chapter 4. Decisions were always made by consensus; the university planner and the staff members from the center acted primarily as advisors, pointing out implications, making suggestions. Most of the design work was done on the site itself, walking around the existing buildings. Drawings were made to record the work we did out on the site; but these drawings were always made *after* decisions had been reached on the site. Designs were not created "on paper."

Here is the sequence of drawings made by the users during that week.

1. This drawing orients the sequence. Existing buildings of the School of Music are outlined.

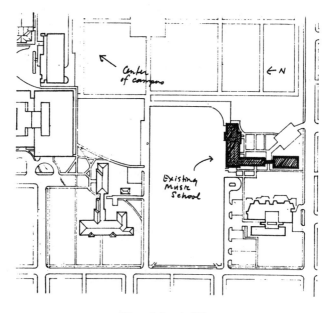

The existing building

2. The Monday drawing establishes possible locations for new buildings. The lines of pedestrian approach are set down. Potential buildings are indicated by blobs, drawn roughly to scale.

Monday

The Tuesday drawing takes the opposite tack. Instead of showing the possible building sites, it locates the possible outdoor sites that could function as small hubs of activity.

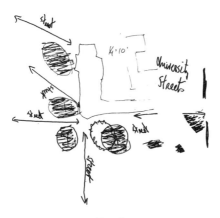

Tuesday

4. On Wednesday the group chose places for buildings, and places for public open spaces. In addition, new functions were assigned to areas in both the old and new buildings. Critical adjacencies, such as the proximity of practice rooms to practice auditoria, were set down.

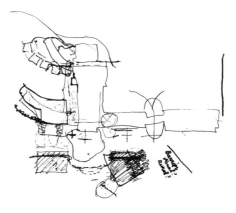

Wednesday

5. The Thursday drawing was made as a result of long hours walking around the site, imagining the exact location of buildings, the feeling of the open spaces, and the clarity of circulation among the various buildings. The buildings were more precisely scaled at this point, and rough space assignments were fixed.

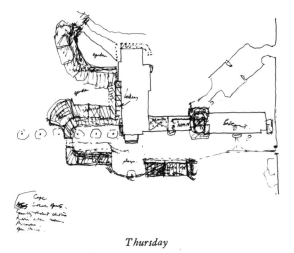

Thursday

6. This is a detailed drawing showing the organization of piano and organ teaching studios.

Thursday afternoon

7. This schematic drawing represents the culmination of the week's efforts. The design, of course, is still far from finished. But it shows what a user group can accomplish in a week of intense design work.

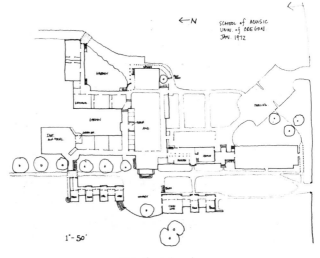

The final drawing

We believe that this design goes a long way to establish the case for participation. The people involved entered fully into the design process; they could make the design what it is only because of their working knowledge of the day-to-day activities and problems of the school. Even though the design is still in its infancy, you can see already how alive and rich it is, how much more love and care there is for every corner—than in the over-simple box-like designs so often churned out in the mid-twentieth century.

The Dean of the Music School, Robert Trotter, talked about the experience of this week of design a few months later, in a local newspaper, AVENU, School of Architecture and Arts, University of Oregon:

. . . Midway through the week everybody experienced a kind of overnight conversion. A kind of "what's going on here?" What is really happening? What have I been doing that I must not be doing, and vice versa? And the same happened to everyone else in the group. So that Wednesday, there was an extraordinary difference in our experience—from Wednesday to Friday afternoon we really went into high gear. . . .

And, for most of us, certainly, it was the first time that we had to deal in spatial terms, in spatial imagery. Also, in a way, rather rare, we began to deal with each other directly—and the experts were not playing cat and mouse with us, but were in effect saying . . . damn it they didn't say: they kept making us realize that it was not so much that they knew exactly what to do and just weren't telling us: it was that the essence of what came out had to be from us.

Let us turn now to the practical implications of our discussion. What steps must be taken in a community like the University of Oregon, where there are a large number of users who are not legal owners of the buildings, to allow these transient users to take an active part in the process of designing buildings? The practical steps needed are expressed by our second principle:

The principle of participation: All decisions about what to build, and how to build it, will be in the hands of the users. To this end, there shall be a users design team for every proposed building project; any group of users may initiate a project, and only those projects initiated by users shall be considered for funding; the planning staff shall give the members of the design team whatever patterns, diagnosis and additional help they need for their design; the time that users need to do a project, shall be treated as a legitimate and essential part of their activities; the design team shall complete their schematic designs before any architect or builder begins to play a major role.

This principle is made more precise by the following details:

(i) *There shall be a users design team for every proposed building project.*

58

We propose that every building, and every increment of building, be designed by a group of users representing a cross-section of the actual or future users of that building. When the group is set up by one person—a director, a dean, an administrator—special care must be taken to insure the right cross-section of representation. If the composition of a project team is disputed by a group who claims representation, the matter goes to the planning board for review. In general, the planning board is the judge of proper user representation.

To make certain that a project group can function, it is necessary to establish an upper limit on the size of the team. Our experience with design teams suggests that this limit should be fixed at six or seven. It is impossible to have a working team, with each member playing a real part, if the group becomes much larger.

Because the groups must be kept small, it is necessary to establish the idea of "visiting" or consultant members of the team. When the design reaches a point that involves the interests of people not present, the group may invite these people in, on an ad hoc basis, to work out some part of the project.

(ii) *Any group of users may initiate a project, and only those projects initiated by users shall be considered for funding.*

It is understood that any group of users, large or small, can propose a project, with equal chances of getting funds. To encourage users to come forward with proposals, we suggest that public announcements calling for proposals be made each year. These announcements make it clear that any group of students, faculty or staff, ad hoc or formally constituted, can propose a project.

Obvious as this idea may seem, it is contrary to current practice. Currently, the initiation of projects comes almost entirely from a handful of people—deans, department chairmen, a few faculty members on special committees, university administrators, and their assistants. Certainly these people have a unique vantage point, and their proposals are worthwhile. But current planning procedures have made such people, de facto, the *only* people with the power to initiate projects. The concept that any group of users—ad hoc or officially established—may initiate projects, on an equal footing, has never been formally encouraged. It is self-evident however, that this concept will yield over the years a far richer, a far more human range of ideas, than the more limited system of initiation which holds today.

(iii) *The planning staff shall give the members of the design team whatever patterns, diagnosis, and additional help they need for their design.*

Any user group which applies to the planning staff will be given a package of information which includes all currently adopted patterns, and the current diagnosis, with all its maps and policies; after discussion, the users decide which patterns and what parts of the diagnosis are applicable to their proposed project; furthermore the group may request help from a member of the planning staff.

The user groups submit a draft of their proposal to the planning staff. The planning staff then works with them, explains any obscure points of the diagnosis or patterns, and helps them prepare a final draft of the project, for formal submission to the planning board.

For details about patterns, diagnosis, and the design process, see chapter 4, 5, and 6, respectively.

(iv) *The time that users need to do a project shall be treated as a legitimate and essential part of their activities.*

In the university, the time which users spend on

planning and designing university buildings must be considered a legitimate part of their teaching and research duties, administrative duties, or course work, according as they are faculty, staff or students. Faculty will be given credit towards their committee duties when they serve on user groups; students will be given credit for course work.

(v) *The design team shall complete their schematic designs before any architect or builder begins to play a major role.*

The process specified allows a user team to develop schematic designs for themselves. In this chapter we have shown that a user group has the capacity to make such designs, when the planning process encourages it. This subprinciple reinforces this point: not only do user groups have the capacity to develop schematic designs for their own environments; it is essential that we learn to make use of this capacity to the utmost. If we were simply to ask the users to state their needs, or make bubble diagrams, and then hand this information over to an architect or a campus planner, we would be losing the real kernel of participation—the fact that users can contribute to a project an essence that normally escapes the professional.

We know however, that the user groups do

need some form of guidance, and encouragement, even though the pattern language does give them the capacity to take charge of the design themselves. How shall they get this guidance?

We foresee hundreds of projects being initiated, by a great variety of user groups, in any given year. Most of these groups will have no access to funds; the generic planning process must not, therefore, *require* funds for outside professionals. Instead, the user groups should be able to get what help they need from the in-house planning staff. In the cases where a project team is able to get outside professional help early in the course of the design, it is essential that they—not the professionals—maintain responsibility for the project until it reaches the schematic stage.

Once a schematic design has been submitted for funding, and approved—at that stage, it will of course be necessary to hire an architect who can prepare a set of contract drawings for construction. To make sure that the architect interprets the schematic design correctly, it is essential that even at that stage, the users who have made the design have the power to hire the architect, and that it is clearly understood that he is responsible for accepting the design which they have made.

A note. We close this chapter with a word about the question of size. The kind of participation which we advocate will not work if individual building projects are too large. People can get involved in the design of small projects—a classroom, outdoor space, a small building, the court between two buildings. But they cannot get involved in the design of large projects—high rise, building complexes, redevelopment projects. There are three reasons.

First, no group of more than about 10 people working together can comfortably undertake a building project. This means that any project which serves more than 10 people is already beyond the immediate reach of some of the users. If the project serves 50 to 100 people, it is possible for everyone to be involved, at least by representation through a friend; no one is removed by more than one step from the process of design. When a project serves more than 100 people, it is clear that design decisions must be made by a group somewhat removed from the people who will live and work in the building. As projects get larger, user representation becomes clumsy, and the building itself tends to be impersonal.

Second, when committees discuss budgets, it has

been found that they spend "far too long" discussing small projects—like the building of a garden fence—and far too little time discussing huge ventures, like the construction of a multi-million dollar factory. The members of the committee can feel personally related to the building of a garden fence, so they have intelligent and reliable intuitions about it and can talk about it. When it comes to the gigantic project, they cannot see themselves personally related to it, so they discuss it very abstractly, and make quick decisions. In short, even at the highest levels of decision-making, people feel remote from the design of huge ventures. It is the small projects which capture their imagination, and emotion, and involvement.

Finally, people will take part only if they feel responsible for their environment; and they feel responsible only if they can identify the parts of the environment which belong to them. Large building projects do much to rob people of this feeling. When large buildings are built, people and departments are treated like objects, and bundles of them are allocated to slots in the buildings, the way crates are allocated to holds inside a cargo ship. Under such conditions, how is it possible to feel any sense of ownership and responsibility? How is it possible to care for one's environment, and make plans to change it?

We see then that participation hinges on the scale of building projects: If the projects are too large, participation is killed. We might have written a clause on the size of the building projects into the principle of participation in this chapter. But there are so many other important reasons for making building projects small, that we have devoted an entire chapter to this subject. The next chapter ends with the principle of piecemeal growth—the principle which guarantees that building projects will be small enough for users to take part in their design.

CHAPTER 3

PIECEMEAL GROWTH

We now come to the idea of piecemeal growth. By piecemeal growth we mean growth that goes forward in small steps, where each project spreads out and adapts itself to the twists and turns of function and site: a small wing added to an old building, to create classrooms and a sunny open space; a small parking lot built in the dead space beside a major road; an arcaded path added to connect two buildings; an outdoor room, covered by a trellis, built in a spot where people often pause and stand in groups; a cafe in a corner of the university where there is no place to sit and study now; each project attuned to the nature of the terrain, the trees, the greens, the character of the surrounding buildings. In this chapter we shall argue that piecemeal growth, like participation, is essential to the creation of organic order.

Let us begin by examining the notion of organic growth and repair. Any living system must repair itself constantly in order to maintain its balance and coordination, its quality as a whole. In the case of an organism, it is only the constant repair, the adjustment of chemical fields, the replacement of cells, and the healing of damaged tissues, which maintain the basic morphology of the organism.

In the case of the environment, the process of growth and repair that is required to maintain morphological integration is far more complex. Repair not only has to conserve a pre-ordained order, as it does in an organism, but must also adapt continuously to changing uses and activities, at every level of scale. For environments, therefore, an organic process of growth and repair must create a gradual sequence of changes, and these changes must be distributed evenly across every level of scale. There must be as much attention to the repair of details—rooms, wings of buildings, windows, paths—as to the creation of brand new buildings. Only then can an environment stay balanced both as a whole, and in its parts, at every moment of its history.

All the good environments that we know have this in common. They are whole and alive because they have grown slowly over long periods

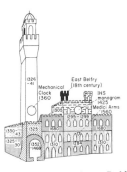

Stages of growth of the Palazzo Publico, Siena

*Piecemeal growth and repair over time—A street in
Canterbury, England*

of time, piece by piece. The pieces are small—and there are always a balanced number of projects going forward at every scale. If one large building is being built, there are, simultaneously, many repairs and changes going forward at smaller scales all around the building; and each new building is not a "finished" thing, but brings in its train a long series of smaller repair projects. In such a way buildings adapt to changing users and changing needs. They are never torn down, never erased; instead they are always embellished, modified, reduced, enlarged, improved. This attitude to the repair of the environment has been commonplace for thousands of years in traditional cultures. We may summarize the point of view behind this attitude in one phrase: *piecemeal growth.*

The importance of piecemeal growth seems obvious. However, obvious or not, it is not a point of view that is widely shared by university architects, administrators, developers, and financiers in 1972.* Instead, most of the people concerned with

---

* The only discussion we know on the importance of piecemeal growth is a beautifully concise article by E.H. Gombrich, "The Beauty of Old Towns," *Architectural Association Journal,* April 1965. Unfortunately this paper seems only to have appeared in a small, relatively unknown journal, and for all practical purposes its message has been lost in the whirl of modern architecture.

*University of Oregon, Science buildings: the result of
a sequence of large lump developments*

university development in the last twenty years,
have taken an almost opposite point of view—a
point of view which we may call *"large lump development."*

In large lump development, the environment
grows in massive chunks. The pieces are often more
than three to four storys high and more than 10
to 20,000 square feet in area. Once a building is
built, it is considered finished; it is not part of a
long sequence of repair projects. These "finished"
buildings are assumed to have a certain finite
lifetime; the process of environmental growth is

seen as a process in which those buildings which have reached the end of their lifetime are torn down, and replaced by new large buildings, again assumed to have a certain lifetime. The fundamental assumption is that it is better to be in a new building than in an old building: and the money spent on the environment is concentrated in the huge new projects, while the money spent maintaining old buildings is reduced to the bare minimum.

We shall now contrast the process of piecemeal growth with the process of large lump development, and try to show that large lump development is worse than piecemeal development in almost every way that matters.

We start with an example from the University of Oregon. The School of Education badly needs more space. In the 1960's a team of administrators and architects, acting according to the University's normal processes, proposed a multi-million dollar complex to replace the existing School of Education, and to house the Departments of Education, Psychology, and Sociology. This complex is a typical example of large lump development. We contrast this large lump scheme with a sketch scheme which shows how the School of Education might be enlarged and modified, according to the policy of piecemeal growth. (We have not shown schemes for the other two departments. Under the piecemeal approach these departments would stay in their own neighborhoods, and be improved in a similar manner.)

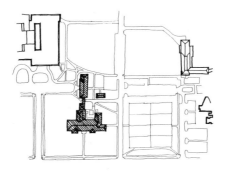

The existing School of Education

What are the most obvious differences between the two schemes? The piecemeal scheme maintains and repairs the places which are working, and which, over the years, have come to have some human character; the large lump development destroys these places and replaces them with a

73

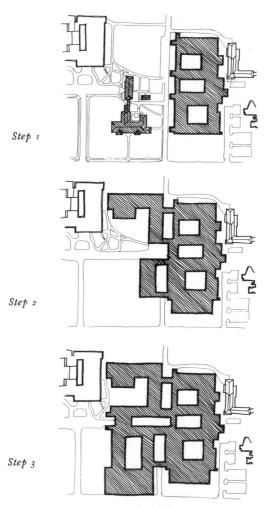

Step 1

Step 2

Step 3

*Large lump development—this wipes out
the existing school*

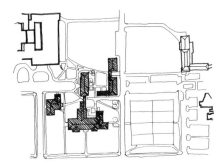

Step 1

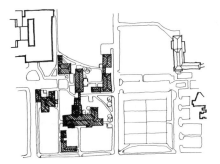

Step 2

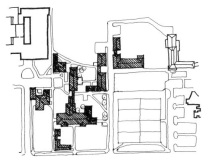

Step 3

*Piecemeal growth—this maintains
the existing school*

75

monolith. The piecemeal scheme finely tunes each new building to the land and the places around it; the other scheme, like a brassy stranger, entirely upsets the scale and fabric of this corner of the campus. And the costs: the large lump project ties up several million dollars in a single act of construction, $2.3 million alone for the School of Education; while the piecemeal scheme spends the money more prudently, in a series of projects, totalling $1.4 million.

The basic philosophical difference between the two approaches is this: *Large lump development hinges on a view of the environment which is static and discontinuous; piecemeal growth hinges on a view of the environment which is dynamic and continuous.*

According to the large lump point of view, each act of design or construction is an isolated event which creates an isolated building—"perfect" at the time of its construction, and then abandoned by its builders and designers forever. According to the piecemeal point of view, every environment is changing and growing all the time, in order to keep its use in balance; and the quality of the environment is a kind of semi-stable equilibrium in the flux of time.

According to the large lump view, since buildings are always built in a vacuum and replaced when obsolete, the environment is seen as an assembly of elements—each one of them *replaceable*. The land between the buildings is naturally seen as a void, "left-over space." According to the piecemeal view, however, the environment is a continuous fabric—which covers all buildings and all outdoor spaces—and the changes which are made within this fabric are merely *repairs* in the totality of the fabric.

Large lump development is based on the idea of *replacement*. Piecemeal growth is based on the idea of *repair*. Since replacement means consumption of resources, while repair means conservation of resources, it is easy to see that piecemeal growth is the sounder of the two from an ecological point of view.

But there are even more practical differences. Large lump development is based on the fallacy that it is possible to build perfect buildings. Piecemeal growth is based on the healthier and more realistic view that mistakes are inevitable. Of course no building is perfect when it is built. It always has mistakes in it. The mistakes show up gradually during the first few years of the building's use. Unless money is available for repairing these mistakes, every building once built, is condemned to be, to some extent, unworkable.

Large lump development works against the possibility of repairing these mistakes. The large projects on a capital construction budget always drive out the small ones, and, in particular, they drive out those very smallest ones which are concerned with making minor corrections in the environment. The administrators responsible for large building projects seem to believe that architects are infallible; they fail to acknowledge the near certainty of error, and therefore fail to set aside any substantial sums of money for repair. Buildings made under the impacts of this kind of thinking fit their users just about as well as a made-to-measure suit would fit its wearer if he refused to go to the tailor for a fitting.

And large lump development works against the possibility of repairing these mistakes in an even more obvious and serious way. Any mistake which is made, is likely to be multiplied by the sheer scale of the buildings—so that it requires a considerable sum of money to correct even a minor mistake. In the College of Environmental Design, at Berkeley, for example, the wrong light fixtures were installed, with the result that the hum of the fluorescent tubes is high enough to make it hard to think throughout the building. Since the building covers 225,000 square feet, the cost of repairing this one tiny mistake would have been $20,000—a sum of money that just was not available—so, seven years after the building was built, people still cannot hear themselves think in their offices and seminar rooms.

In piecemeal growth the mistakes are smaller to begin with. Indeed, within the context of piecemeal growth, it is perhaps even misleading to call them mistakes. Piecemeal growth is based on the assumption that adaptation between buildings and their users is necessarily a slow and continuous business which cannot, under any circumstances, be achieved in a single leap. And it is understood, therefore, that a little money must be set aside, for every part of a community, in every year, so that the adaptation can keep going, everywhere, as a continuous process.

In a community with a centralized budget, like the University of Oregon, the large lump development has another, even more serious consequence. Since the single, overall budget is limited, the various groups within the community are in competition for the funds. They know that only one or two projects will get funded in any given budget year, and therefore know that they will have to make a very strong case indeed to get one of these highly prized projects. This means that each group enormously exaggerates its needs, which enlarges their projects artificially and makes it even less likely that other groups can get any money. In short, once the process of large lump development has started, its internal dynamics make the lumps larger and larger all the time, as the different groups exaggerate more and more wildly to win the competition for projects.

The larger the projects get, the more dissatisfied the users must inevitably be. Under large lump development, no one department can hope for construction funds more often than once in every twenty or thirty years. Since buildings never fit their inhabitants perfectly just after they are built, the departments are left in a sorry situation: they cannot institute a rhythm of repair that will gradually fit the building to them; they have no hope of meeting their needs in the foreseeable future. So long as large lump development is going on, this is the situation for most of the departments, most of the time. They are stuck with what they have; and when they finally do have a chance to do something about it, they again put all their eggs into one huge basket, and then again spend the next twenty years living with the inadequacies of their latest mistakes.

In piecemeal growth, everything is more modest. It is not necessary for people to exaggerate their needs, because money is used only for needs which actually exist, right now. This reduces the total annual need so radically that it makes enough money available to provide for all those needs which actually occur, *when they occur,* no later. The allocations are spread out; every place is being improved, bit by bit, year after year.

The uneven character of large lump development works against the possibilities of creating balance in one more way. It makes virtually certain that large parts of the community will become slums. This follows naturally from the fact that all the available money is always being gathered together to pay for the newest large buildings: there are never regular and substantial sums of money left over for the buildings which are *not* currently under construction, and therefore there are always large parts of the environment which are chronically under-maintained.

Parts of cities have gradually become slums for somewhat similar reasons. The money goes into huge development projects, in the areas where land is cheap; old parts of the city are left to decay; there is nothing to be "gained" by improving them. Though they do not seem to go downhill so fast, many campuses are today faced with a similar prospect. Originally there was a center. The center gets old and run down about the same time that new complexes are built up on the periphery. But the cost of new construction is vast, so the repair required to revitalize the old center is passed over. The more it runs down, the less inviting it becomes; eventually it becomes a slum.

At the University of Oregon, two decades of large lump development have left the campus in just this state. A recent report on the University of Oregon in the Eugene *Register-Guard* estimated that "half of the buildings on campus need to be replaced, and another 10 per cent are in need of major rehabilitation." If the present policy of large lump development continues for another two decades, it will almost certainly make parts of the University of Oregon a slum by 1990.

In order to take care of the University as a whole, we must take care of *all* of it, all of the

Science Library Court: The beginning of a slum. This mistake, because it is part of a large lump development, cannot be repaired. There is no money left.

time. What this means is that the available resources must be spent in a way which distributes the improvements uniformly over the space of the university. To put this in extreme, but graphic terms, it means that when we have one dollar to spend, we should spend it evenly, across the board, so that every square foot of the campus gets the same percentage of this dollar.

Piecemeal growth comes much closer to this idea than large lump development. Each year a little money is spent on parking, a little on improving student housing, a little on improving the lecture halls, a little on improving the outdoor places, a little on each of the academic buildings. Slowly, but surely, the university environment improves; the old places are not left to rot. As the development goes forward on all fronts at once, gradually the various pieces of development will come to form a whole.

For all these reasons, piecemeal growth works to create organic order; large lump development tends to break it down.

One doubt remains: perhaps piecemeal growth costs more. One of the reasons often given for the huge scale of buildings built under large lump development is that they are cheaper. If this were true, piecemeal growth might be too expensive to be practical.

In the following pages we shall try to establish that the supposed cost savings of large buildings are mythical. Small buildings cost no more, per net usable square foot, than large buildings. In fact, we have found that cost of construction generally increases with size and height of buildings.

First of all, large buildings require more expensive types of construction. Table 1 shows the

84

types of construction required to satisfy the Uniform Building Code for school buildings of varying sizes, ranging from 5000 to 130,000 square feet; and heights ranging from one story to eight stories. Since different types of construction have different expected lives, we correct the raw costs by adding the present cost of replacing the structure when its useful life expires (Table 1, Column 7). Even when we add this correction, we see that small buildings still cost less per square foot, than large ones.

The other big increases in the cost of large buildings come from the loss of usable interior space, the provision of elevators, and a 1 per cent increase in cost for the construction of each additional story. The 1 per cent addition is based on procedures for estimating construction costs given in the Marshall and Stevens Valuation Handbook, 1970. The loss of usable space in high buildings is due to additional corridors, lobbies, elevators, and space given over to mechanical equipment. To calculate these losses we applied percentages based on data provided by Skidmore, Owings and Merrill (Table 2, Column 3). The overall cost comparisons are given in Table 2.

85

TABLE 1. Cost per gross square foot for different types of construction

size of building	no. of stories	construction type code B	construction description A	life of structure	sq. ft. cost B	cost for reduced life C	total sq. ft. cost
5,000	1	V no hour	Wood frame or pipe columns	35	$14.78	$3.68	$18.46
10,000	1	IV no hour	Steel frame or bearing walls, brick, block, or concrete	40	16.29	1.62	17.91
15,000	2	IV 1 hour	Steel columns, web or bar joists, block brick or concrete	50	19.90	0	19.90
20,000	2	II	Steel or concrete, 2 hr. fire proofing	50	22.50	0	22.50
30,000	3	II	" "		22.50	0	22.50
40,000	3	I	Steel or concrete, 4 hr. fire proofing	50	24.00	0	24.00
50,000	4	I	" "	50	24.00	0	24.00
60,000	4	I	" "	50	24.00	0	24.00
70,000	5	I	" "	50	24.00	0	24.00
80,000	5	I	" "	50	24.00	0	24.00
90,000	6	I	" "	50	24.00	0	24.00
100,000	6	I	" "	50	24.00	0	24.00
110,000	7	I	" "	50	24.00	0	24.00
120,000	7	I	" "	50	24.00	0	24.00
130,000	8	I	" "	50	24.00	0	24.00

A From the Uniform Building Code.
B Costs taken from Marshall and Stevens Valuation Service, 1970.
C Value added for reduced life is calculated by assuming that a similar structure would be provided at the end of its life for a 15 year period and then discounted at 6% to its present value.

TABLE 2. Cost per square foot of net useable space

size of building	no. of stories	% net useable space A	total net sq. ft.	cost per gross sq. ft. B	gross total cost	add cost of elevators C	total building costs D	cost per net sq. ft.
5,000	1	90%	4,500	$18.46	92,300	NA	92,300	$20.51
10,000	1	90%	9,000	17.91	179,100	"	179,100	19.90
15,000	2	90%	13,500	19.90	298,500	"	298,500	22.11
20,000	2	90%	18,000	22.50	450,000	"	450,000	25.00
30,000	3	90%	27,000	22.73	681,900	(2)131,000	812,900	30.11
40,000	3	88%	35,200	24.25	970,000	(2)131,000	1,101,000	31.28
50,000	4	86%	43,000	24.50	1,225,000	(3)202,000	1,427,000	33.18
60,000	4	85%	51,000	24.50	1,470,000	(3)202,000	1,672,000	32.80
70,000	5	84%	58,800	24.75	1,732,500	(4)269,000	2,001,500	34.04
80,000	5	83%	66,400	24.75	1,980,000	(4)269,000	2,249,000	33.87
90,000	6	82%	73,800	25.00	2,250,000	(5)353,000	2,603,000	35.27
100,000	6	81%	81,000	25.00	2,500,000	(5)353,000	2,853,000	35.22
110,000	7	80%	88,000	25.25	2,777,500	(5)353,000	3,130,500	35.57
120,000	7	80%	96,000	25.25	3,030,000	(6)433,000	3,463,000	36.07
130,000	8	80%	104,000	25.50	3,315,000	(6)433,000	3,748,000	36.04

A From interview with Skidmore, Owings, and Merrill, San Francisco.
B From Table I plus 1% addition for each extra story.
C These cost are based on Marshall and Stevens Valuation Service: $60,750 per shaft, 500 feet per minute, 3000 lb. capacity. $1625 is added for each stop. Number of elevators provided is based on assumption of 1 elevator for every 150 persons residing in the building.
D Rounded to hundreds.

The following two graphs summarize the relation between building size and cost. First, the relation between building height and the cost per square foot of net usable space: as we see, the cost increases with height.

Cost versus height

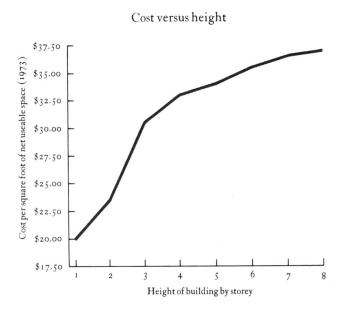

Second, the relation between gross area of construction and the cost per square foot of net usable space: as we see, the cost increases sharply when buildings reach a gross area of 20,000 square feet or more.

88

Cost versus size

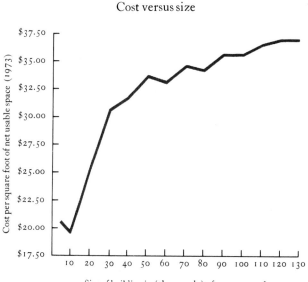

Size of building in (thousands) of gross square feet

To test these results further, Larry Bissett, the campus planner, gathered building cost data on seventy-two school buildings from many areas within the state of Oregon. The samples include buildings constructed through the State Board of Higher Education as well as local high school and elementary school districts. The cost per square foot is based on gross square feet, since net usable figures were not available. However, even without taking into account the higher gross/net ratio characteristic of larger buildings, we find the aver-

89

age cost per gross square foot, for three different size categories, to be about equal. The results are presented in Table 3.

TABLE 3. Cost per gross square foot
versus size of building

size	average cost	no. of buildings sampled
0–15,000 square feet	$22.13	16
15–35,000 " "	23.39	20
35,000 + " "	23.35	36

Information from other countries supports our findings. In several cases it has been shown that construction of a given amount of floor space in a high-rise building is more expensive than the construction of the same amount in a low-rise building.

In England, for example, these calculations have resulted in the recent withdrawal of subsidies to high-rise residential construction. The British Ministry of Housing and Local Government took this stand after it became clear that high rise buildings are more expensive than three to four story buildings. (Ministry of Housing and Local Government, *Circular No. 36/37*, London, 1968.) Another English study has shown that the cost per square meter of usable floor area increases steadily with height. (Thomas Sharp, *Towns and Townscape*, London, 1968, p. 132. Sharp's study is based on tables prepared by P. A. Stone, "Economics of Housing Urban Development," *Journal of the Royal Statistical Society*, [Series A], Vol. 122, 1958; and Nathaniel Lichfield, "Net Density, Cost and Value in Public Authority Dwellings," *The Chartered Surveyor*, September, 1960, pp. 3–11.)

In addition to the increase in construction costs, there is also a steep increase in the *maintenance cost* of high buildings. In Glasgow, for example, it was found that the maintenance cost per housing unit in a low building was 8.39 pounds in 1970, while the maintenance cost for a housing unit in a multi-story building that same year was 21.35 pounds (Pearl Jephcott with Hilary Robinson, *Homes in High Flats; Some of the human problems involved in multi-storey housing*, University of Glasgow, Edinburgh, 1971, p. 128.)

We can safely conclude that the small projects created by the piecemeal growth approach will cost no more per net usable square foot than the projects created by large lump development, and may perhaps cost less.

It remains to ask what practical measures will help to implement the process of piecemeal growth.

At first sight, it might seem as though a simple ceiling on the size of any given project might be sufficient. For example: "No one project may cost more than $500,000." However, a moment's thought will make it clear that this is not workable. It is both too low and too high. On the one hand, there can always be some project—a freeway tunnel, for example—which would cost several million dollars, and cannot be built in increments. In this sense, $500,000 is too low. On the other hand, $500,000 also fails to reflect the fact that we want the great majority of projects to cost far *less* than half a million—more like a few thousand dollars each. In this sense $500,000 is far too high.

Instead of specifying a ceiling on project size, we must specify the distribution of project sizes—the total proportion of the budget which should be spent on projects of different sizes. This is captured by the following principle:

The principle of piecemeal growth: The construction undertaken in each budgetary period will be weighted overwhelmingly toward small proj-

ects. To this end, in any given budgetary period, equal sums shall be spent on large, medium, and small building projects, so as to guarantee the numerical predominance of very small building increments; when funds come from outside the community, as they do at the University of Oregon, the government which supplies these funds must support this principle, by earmarking funds for large, medium, and small projects in equal proportions; in the small project category, the government must release its funds as lump sums, without regard for the specific details of individual projects.

(i) *In any given budgetary period, equal sums shall be spent on large, medium, and small building projects, so as to guarantee the numerical predominance of very small building increments.*

Consider any system of budget categories, which classifies building projects according to size. Here is an example of a system of categories:

A. Less than $1000

B. $1000–$10,000

C. $10,000–$100,000

D. $100,000–$1,000,000

E. More than $1,000,000

In large lump development there are a few large projects, a few medium sized projects, and a few small projects. The total amount of money spent on small projects is vastly greater than the total amount spent on small projects. *The number of projects in each category is the same.*

TABLE 4. The distribution of projects in a two and a half million dollar budget for large lump development

category	number of projects	rough total cost based on averages
A < $1000	1	500
B $1000–$10,000	1	5,000
C $10,000–$100,000	1	50,000
D $100,000–$1,000,000	1	500,000
E > $1,000,000	1	2,000,000
		$2,500,000

In piecemeal growth, every project of a given size has a number of smaller projects to support it, to fill in the cracks, to help make adjustments in places which are not exactly right. Crudely, but concretely, we may put this as follows: Any one project of $1,000,000 is accompanied by 10 projects which cost $100,000, by 100 projects which cost $10,000 and so on. *The total amount of money spent in each category is the same.*

TABLE 5. The distribution of projects in a two and a half million dollar budget for piecemeal growth

category	number of projects	rough total cost based on averages
A < $1000	1000	500,000
B $1000–$10,000	100	500,000
C $10,000–$100,000	10	500,000
D $100,000–$1,000,000	1	500,000
E > $1,000,000	1/10 of a project	500,000
		$2,500,000

It is plain from the foregoing tables that we can guarantee piecemeal growth, by specifying the distribution of project sizes in a typical budget, category by category. The only question is: exactly what categories should we choose; and exactly what distribution should we specify?

The simplest specification requires that the *total* amount of money devoted to large projects, medium projects, and small projects, is the same. This creates the kind of distribution given in Table 5.

Another milder version of the same principle allows the total amounts of money spent on projects in the large categories to be slightly larger than in the smaller categories. For example, see Table 6.

TABLE 6. Another way of breaking down a two and a half million dollar budget to guarantee piecemeal growth

category	number of projects	rough total cost based on averages
A < $1000	500	250,000
B $1000–$10,000	50	250,000
C $10,000–$100,000	10	500,000
D $100,000–$1,000,000	1	500,000
E > $1,000,000	1	1,000,000
		$2,500,000

We are not yet sure exactly which way of specifying piecemeal growth is best. It requires further research, based on some empirical estimate of the distribution of projects needed to maintain any community in a state of health. In the absence of this research, we recommend for the time being, that some version of this last kind of specification be adopted.

(ii) *When funds come from outside the community, as they do at the University of Oregon, the government which supplies these funds must support this principle, by earmarking funds for large, medium, and small projects in equal proportions.*

In the case of Oregon, the State Board of Higher Education and the Ways and Means Committee of the State Government must understand the importance of this principle, and allocate their own funds in a manner consistent with it. It is important to realize that this demands a radical reversal of the policy that normally guides the State Ways and Means Committee. The present policy seems neutral. In fact it is not: and until the policy changes, the State Ways and Means Committee is, without intending it, an unwitting partner in the process of overspending and large lump development.

Let us understand the mechanism of this unwitting partnership. The State Ways and Means Committee makes no explicit requests for large projects. However, the very fact that they review projects in such detail, means that the State Board, which amalgamates projects from different universities, and submits them to the Ways and Means Committee, has a natural inclination to make the list of projects fairly short. It has to, because otherwise the members of the Ways and Means Committee would not have time to get through the list.

The very fact that this list has to be so short, already tends to make projects relatively large. But beyond that, it happens to be a fact—soon observed by the university and other agencies which ask for funds—that no one institution ever gets funds for more than one or two projects on a given budget list. Once again this follows more or less naturally from the fact that the Ways and Means Committee tries hard to be fair and reasonable, and to spread their available funds more or less equally among the competing campuses.

This fact makes it more or less inevitable that the projects which actually get funded, will be the very largest and most expensive. The reason is simple. The university is trying to get as much money as it possibly can from the State budget. They know that, at least under present conditions, they will get funds for one or two projects only. Naturally, the projects highest on the list have the best chance of being funded, since these are presumed to be most "urgent." So the university authorities naturally put those projects which cost the most at the top of the list, since this gives them the best chance of obtaining a really large sum of money from the state government.

This is how the State Ways and Means Committee is an unwitting partner to large lump development. So long as they maintain their present attitude to the distribution of funds, it actually is in the university's best interest to press for large projects; and it is therefore inevitable, as we have shown, that the university environment will gradually deteriorate.

(iii) *In the small project category, the government must release its funds as lump sums, without regard for the specific details of individual projects.*

At present, every proposed building project is examined in detail by the Ways and Means Committee of the State of Oregon, before receiving funds. For large projects, costing hundreds of thousands or millions of dollars, we believe that this is appropriate, since, within the frame of reference we propose, such large projects will be comparatively unusual anyway, and need to be examined to make certain they are valid.

However, we believe that for smaller projects this practice must stop. In order to implement the policy of piecemeal growth, the Committee must recognize that they cannot examine every small building project in detail before it receives funds —there are just too many of them.

There is a further argument, which supports the same conclusion. The process of project approval may take as long as two years to pass through the full sequence of steps which precede funding approval by the Ways and Means Committee. This is much too long to wait for a small project.

When a group proposes a small project, we may assume that it is a direct, intimate response to some small scale problem, and that they are anxious to act on it immediately. Repairing the department hearth; building a foot bridge across the creek; creating an outdoor classroom; modifying a road; laying down bike paths; repairing a laboratory. People who try to take responsibility for projects like these will not be willing to wait one or two years to find out if they have been approved for funding. The essence of such a project is its immediacy; if the spontaneity is crushed by long periods of waiting and review, these projects will die. Since they are an essential part of the piecemeal process, the state government must recognize their importance, and be willing to release funds for these small projects in lump sum packages, without attention to the details of individual projects, and without the usual lengthy waiting times.

CHAPTER 4

PATTERNS

We now move on to the concepts which will guide the design of buildings within the process of piecemeal growth: the patterns themselves.

Let us begin with a brief definition of a pattern, remembering that from our present point of view, the essential feature which every pattern has, is that it forms the basis for a shared agreement in a community. Each one is, therefore, a statement of some general planning principle so formulated that its correctness, or incorrectness, can be supported by empirical evidence, discussed in public, and then, according to the outcome of these discussions, adopted, or not, by a planning board which speaks for the whole community.

With this in mind, we may define a pattern as any general planning principle, which states a clear problem that may occur repeatedly in the environment, states the range of contexts in which this problem will occur, and gives the general features required by all buildings or plans which solve this problem. In this sense, then, we may regard a pattern as an empirically grounded imperative, which states the preconditions for healthy individual and social life in a community. The exact definition of "health" or "wholeness," and the way in which these very complex concepts can be anchored in empirical realities, the way that many patterns coalesce to form a pattern language, the structure of pattern languages, the processes by which individuals and communities can use a pattern language, and the fact that a shared pattern language is the heart and soul of any successful process of community, are given in *The Timeless Way of Building*.

Further, an actual pattern language, which contains all the patterns necessary for an entire community—at least in one coherent version—is presented in full in *A Pattern Language*. It contains some 250 patterns ranging in scale from large regional patterns, all the way down to the details of construction.

In this chapter, we are now concerned with the specific administrative and democratic mechanisms which will allow a shared pattern language to grow up, naturally, at the University of Oregon

—and which will allow the people to improve this pattern language year after year, until it properly reflects their communal situation, and their communal needs. The practical questions, then, concern the process by which patterns can be shared, and adopted, tentatively, by the university community; the process by which these adopted patterns can be challenged and improved, in later years; and the process by which members of the university community—especially faculty and students—can undertake experiments and observations to improve the patterns.

Let us begin by asking how a community like the University of Oregon can build a pattern language for itself. We imagine that every community which hopes to adopt a common pattern language will find it easiest to start with the second volume of this series: *A Pattern Language*. Of course not all of its 250 patterns will apply: many may be inappropriate, some may be wrong. But the pattern language is so constructed that it is very easy to adapt it to the needs of any local community.

It is easy to adapt, because the 250 patterns which it contains are independent; that is, they make sense one at a time; any collection of them makes sense; and it is possible to add any number of other, newly invented patterns to such a collection, and it will still make sense. This is, in fact, how we propose that a community should start to develop a pattern language for itself.

Let us now take the University of Oregon, as an example. When we look through *A Pattern Language*, we find that about 200 of the 250 patterns are relevant to the university community. About 160 of these 200 deal with building interiors, rooms, gardens, and building construction. These 160 patterns are very important indeed; but, since they do not deal with global problems which affect everyone, it seems better not to adopt them formally, but instead, to treat them as patterns which every user group might use or not use, according to their own instincts, when they design their projects.

However, 37 of the 200 patterns relevant to the university are so large in scale that individual projects will not be able to complete them—and they will only appear at all if many different individual projects help to create them, in cooperation. For this, of course, there must be university-wide agreement about these patterns. These 37 patterns must therefore be formally considered by the planning board, adopted on behalf of the university community, and then, in some fashion, backed by incentives so that individual projects help to make them appear. They are:

LOCAL TRANSPORT AREA
NETWORK OF LEARNING
IDENTIFIABLE
   NEIGHBORHOOD
FOUR STORY LIMIT
ACCESS TO WATER
MINI BUSES
PROMENADE
ACTIVITY NODES
LOOPED LOCAL ROADS
T JUNCTIONS
PATH NETWORK
ROAD CROSSING
QUIET BACKS
ACCESSIBLE GREEN
SMALL PUBLIC SQUARES
DEGREES OF PUBLICNESS
LOCAL SPORTS
SMALL PARKING LOTS

SHIELDED PARKING
PATHS AND GOALS
BIKE PATHS AND RACKS
PATH SHAPE
PEDESTRIAN DENSITY
PUBLIC OUTDOOR ROOM
OFFICE CONNECTIONS
NUMBER OF STORYS
BUILDING COMPLEX
SITE REPAIR
TREE PLACES
SOUTH FACING OUTDOORS
CONNECTED BUILDINGS
MAIN GATEWAYS
MAIN ENTRANCE
FAMILY OF ENTRANCES
WINGS OF LIGHT
POSITIVE OUTDOOR SPACE
ARCADES

This list of 37 patterns is extremely general: It deals with problems of density, buildings, open space, roads, and paths. It does not deal with the specific problems that a university confronts. And yet, of course, these special university problems are as vital to the well being of the environment as the more general ones. It just happens that *A Pattern Language* does not deal with them, precisely because they are too special, too detailed, too local to be included there. We have, therefore, derived 18 special patterns to solve those more specific problems which are peculiar to universities. Every particular community will always need to do the same to supplement the general patterns from *A Pattern Language*. The patterns are:

UNIVERSITY POPULATION
OPEN UNIVERSITY
STUDENT HOUSING DISTRIBUTION
UNIVERSITY SHAPE AND DIAMETER
UNIVERSITY STREETS
LIVING LEARNING CIRCLE
FABRIC OF DEPARTMENTS
DEPARTMENTS OF 400
DEPARTMENT SPACE
LOCAL ADMINISTRATION
STUDENT COMMUNITY
SMALL STUDENT UNIONS
PARKING SPACES
CLASSROOM DISTRIBUTION
FACULTY STUDENT MIX
STUDENT WORKPLACE
REAL LEARNING IN CAFES
DEPARTMENT HEARTH

When we interleave the two lists of patterns, we get a single list of 55 patterns which are global enough for the university to adopt formally. Space prevents us from presenting all these patterns here, in full; however, we consider it vital for the reader to understand how these two lists of patterns interleave to form a single coherent list; and vital also to understand how these large scale formally adopted patterns actually have the power to generate a healthy university environment. For this reason, we shall now present a number of pattern summaries, which include all 18 patterns special to the University of Oregon, and a few (14 of the 37) from *A Pattern Language,* to show the rough scope and content of this list, and what the university gains by adopting this list formally, as the backbone of its planning process.

We want to emphasize the fact that the few pages printed here contain only *summaries* of the 32 patterns, not full texts. The full text of a pattern always describes the empirical evidence behind the pattern. The summaries printed here contain such a brief statement of the problem, that there is no room at all for this empirical evidence which is the cornerstone of any properly formulated pattern. The full texts are either in *A Pattern*

Language, or in the files of the planning office of
the University of Oregon.

I. UNIVERSITY POPULATION

If a university is too small, it suffers from lack of
variety; if it is too large, it no longer works as a
human organization; if it grows too fast, it breaks
down because it doesn't have the chance to absorb
or adjust to change.

Therefore: Limit the growth of any university
to a rate of 2 per cent per year, and limit the
absolute size of any university to 25,000 students.

Data in the University of Oregon files

2. OPEN UNIVERSITY

When a university is built up as a campus, sepa-
rated by a hard boundary from the town, it tends
to isolate its students from the townspeople, and
in a subtle way takes on the character of a glorified
high school.

Therefore: Encourage the dissolution of the
boundary between university and town. Encourage
parts of the town to grow up within the university,
and parts of the university to grow up within the
town.

*Data in a Pattern language and
in the Oregon files*

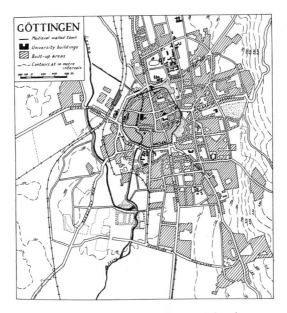

*An open university: Göttingen. University
buildings are shown in black.*

3. STUDENT HOUSING DISTRIBUTION

When students live too far from campus, they cannot be part of university life.

Therefore: Locate all student housing within
a one mile radius of the center of the university
in the following proportions: 25 per cent integrated with academic activities within a 1500 foot
radius of the center (See *Living learning circle*);

25 per cent in a ring between 1500 and 2500 feet of the center; 50 per cent in a ring between 2500 and 5000 feet of the center.

Data in the Oregon files

4. UNIVERSITY SHAPE AND DIAMETER

When a university is too spread out, people cannot make use of all it offers; on the other hand, a diameter for the university based strictly on the 10 minute class break is needlessly restrictive.

Therefore: Plan all classes, evenly distributed, within a circular zone not more than 3000 feet in diameter. Place non-class activities such as athletic fields, research offices, administration within a wider circle, not more than 5000 feet in diameter.

Data in the Oregon files

5. LOCAL TRANSPORT AREA

The impact of the car on social life is devastating: it keeps us off the streets and far away from each other. The first step in bringing the car under control is to stop using it for local trips.

Therefore: Embed the university in a local transport area, 1 to 2 miles in diameter. Within this area, except for very special cases, encourage local trips to be made on foot, bikes, scooters, carts, perhaps even on horseback. Adapt paths and roads to these modes of travel, and keep the streets for cars slow and circuitous. At the edge of the local transport area build high speed ring roads.

Data in Pattern language

Inside a local transport area

6. NINE PER CENT PARKING

When the area devoted to parking is too great it destroys the land.

Therefore: Divide the campus into sectors, and keep the area of parking lots and garages to less than 9 per cent of the land, in every sector.

Data in Pattern language

Parking held at 9 per cent: University of Oregon

7. LOOPED LOCAL ROADS

Through traffic destroys the tranquility and the safety of pedestrian areas. This is especially true in university districts, where the creation of quiet precincts is crucial to the work.

Therefore: To bring the traffic and the pedestrian world into the right balance, make the local roads that serve the area form a system of loops or cul-de-sacs, so that through traffic is impossible.

Data in Pattern language

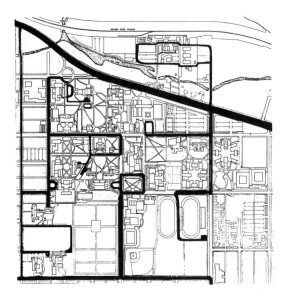

Proposal for looped local roads at the University of Oregon

8. UNIVERSITY STREETS

Large agglomerations of departments and heavily centralized academic facilities kill variety, academic freedom, and student opportunities for learning.

Therefore: Concentrate the major functions of the university—the offices, labs, lecture halls, sports, student quarters—along university streets; streets that are public and essentially pedestrian, 20 to 30 feet wide, with all the university activity

113

opening off them; always locate new buildings to amplify and extend the university streets.

Data in Oregon files and in Pattern language
under Pedestrian street

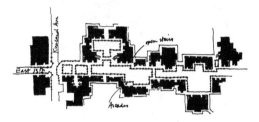

A university street proposed for the University of Oregon

9. LIVING LEARNING CIRCLE

Students who want to live closely related to the university want their housing integrated with the university; yet most on-campus housing provided today is zoned off from academic departments.

Therefore: Provide housing for 25 per cent of the student population within the 3000 foot inner university diameter. Do not zone this housing off from academic departments—instead alternate the two so that there are never more than two or three student communities, nor more than 300 feet of academic functions, before each is interrupted by the other.

Data in Oregon files

10. ACTIVITY NODES

When buildings are spread evenly across a campus, they do not generate small centers of public life around them. They do nothing to help the various "neighborhoods" on the campus to coalesce.

Therefore: When locating buildings, place them in conjunction with other buildings to form small nodes of public life. Create a series of these nodes throughout the university, in contrast to the quiet, private outdoor spaces between them, and knit these nodes together with a network of pedestrian paths.

Data in Pattern language

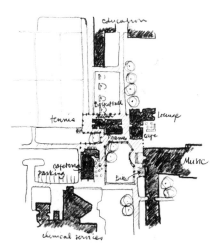

An activity node proposed for University of Oregon

11. ACCESSIBLE GREEN

When people work extremely close to large open green areas, they visit them and use them often; but even a fairly short distance will discourage them.

Therefore: Provide a green outdoor park, at least 60,000 square feet in area, at least 150 feet across in the narrowest direction, within 600 feet of every building in the university.

Data in Pattern language

Accessible green at the University of Virginia

12. FABRIC OF DEPARTMENTS

Over-emphasis on the individuality of departments helps to fragment knowledge by keeping it in watertight compartments. Yet each department does require its own identity.

Therefore: Give each department a clearly identified home base, but spread the parts of the department within a radius of 500 feet, so that they interlock with the parts of other departments. No one of these parts should contain less than five faculty offices.

Data in Oregon files

13. DEPARTMENTS OF 400
When a department is too large, students and faculty become alienated; it becomes hard to run successful programs there; and hard to maintain the proper educational milieu.

Therefore: Limit the size of any university department. Our current best estimate for the tolerable maximum is 400 students plus faculty. When departments grow beyond this size, they must be split to form new departments.

Data in Oregon files

The growth of a new department

14. DEPARTMENT SPACE

Spaces are not working properly if they are over-crowded or if they are under-used. Empty desolate spaces are as bad to work in as overcrowded ones.

Therefore: Give each department approximately ($160A + 80B + 55C$) square feet of net usable space, where A is the number of faculty, B is the number of staff, and C is the number of graduate students and students who live more than one mile from the university. Laboratories and classrooms must be figured separately.

Full details and data in Oregon files

15. LOCAL ADMINISTRATION

University administrative services are often over-centralized: all the branches are located together in one imposing complex, when, in fact, various parts of administration could operate more effectively if they were located according to the functional connections each requires in the community.

Therefore: Locate different administrative services independently, each one as near as possible to the center of gravity of its particular community (e.g., Dean of Students in the Student Union; counseling near student housing). Never create one vast administrative territory for all the services.

Data in Oregon files

16. STUDENT COMMUNITY

If dormitories are too small and too communal, they become constraining. If they are too big or too private, then the idea of group living is lost.

Therefore: Encourage the formation of autonomously managed cooperative housing clusters that bring 30 to 40 units together, around communal eating, sports, etc. Unlike dorms, however, make the individual units rather autonomous, with sink, toilet and hot plates, and with private entrances.

Data in Oregon files

Old student clubhouse, University of California, Berkeley

17. SMALL STUDENT UNIONS

When a single building on campus is designated as student territory, it raises the feeling that the rest of campus is not student territory.

Therefore: Create many small student unions across campus—one for every 500 to 1000 students, and so placed that there are no classrooms or offices farther than two minutes from the nearest one. Give each small center at least a coffee bar and lounge/reading room, and an area of roughly 2.5N square feet, where N is the number of people it serves.

Data in Oregon files

18. BUILDING COMPLEX

When human organizations are housed in enormous buildings, the human scale vanishes, and people stop identifying with the staff who work there as personalities, and think only of the entire institution as an impersonal monolith, staffed with "personnel."

Therefore: To maintain human scale in public buildings, make them small, not more than 3 to 4 storeys high; not more than 9000 square feet in total indoor area; not more than 3000 square feet to a story. If more than one small building is being made, to house related functions, the buildings should be conceived as a collection, connected by arcades, paths, bridges.

Data in Pattern language under Four story limit
and Building Complex

*Building complex—Anna Head School,
Berkeley, California*

19. CIRCULATION REALMS

In many modern public buildings, and in many parts of cities, the problem of disorientation is acute. People have no idea where they are, and they experience considerable mental stress as a result.

Therefore: Arrange buildings so that it is possible to identify a nested system of realms in every building complex, so clearly marked that every realm has an identity that can be named; and give each realm at every level a clearly marked entrance.

Data in Pattern language

Gateway to circulation realms

20. SOUTH FACING OUTDOOR SPACE

People use open space if it is sunny, and don't use it if it isn't, in all but desert climates.

Therefore: Place buildings so that the open space intended for use is on the south side of the buildings; avoid putting open space in the shadow of buildings; and never let a deep strip of shade separate a sunny area from the building which it serves.

Data in Pattern language

Courtyard oriented to the sun, Taliesin,
Spring Green, Wisconsin

21. POSITIVE OUTDOOR SPACE

Outdoor spaces which are merely "left over" between buildings will, in general, not be used.

Therefore: Always place buildings, arcades, trees,
and walls, so that the outdoor spaces they form
are convex in plan. But never enclose an outdoor
space on all sides—instead connect outdoor spaces

to one another so that it is possible to see and walk from one to the next in more than one way.

Data in Pattern language

Positive open space

22. WINGS OF LIGHT

The excessive use of artificial light in modern buildings is inhuman; buildings which displace natural light as the major source of illumination are not fit places to spend the day.

Therefore: Limit the width of buildings to 30 feet and make up larger buildings from several 30 foot wide wings.

Data in Pattern language

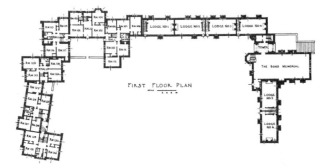

FIRST FLOOR PLAN

Wings of light—Women's Quad,
Swarthmore College

23. PARKING SPACES

As the university grows, there is a great danger that parking will overwhelm the university environment. But if the parking is too far away, it can easily degrade teaching and learning.

Therefore: For every building with N staff offices and M workstations, provide $0.25M$ metered short term spaces, 300 feet from the building, in the direction away from the university center; and $N(0.67 - 0.57P)$ commuter spaces 500 feet away from the building, also in the direction away from the university center, where P is the percentage of staff who live within 15 minutes walk.

Data in Oregon files

24. SMALL PARKING LOTS

Vast parking lots wreck the land for people.

Therefore: Make parking lots small, for 8 to 12 cars; when a lot requires more parking, build it up as a collection of these 8 to 12 car lots, along a spine, each lot bounded and enclosed with wall, hedge, trees; not visible from the outside.

Data in Pattern language

Small parking lot, Cambridge

25. BIKE PATHS AND RACKS

Bikes are cheap, healthy, and good for the environment; but they are threatened by cars on major roads; and they threaten pedestrians on pedestrian paths.

Therefore: Build a system of paths designated as "bike paths," with the following properties: The bike paths are marked clearly with a special, easily recognizable surface (for example, a red asphalt surface). Bike paths always coincide either with local roads, or major pedestrian paths. Where the system coincides with a local road, its surface may simply be part of the road and level with it. Where the system coincides with a pedestrian path, the bike path is separate from that path and a few inches below it. The system of bike paths comes within 100 feet of every building, and every build- has a bike rack near its main entrance.

Data in Pattern language

A bike path in France

26. LOCAL SPORTS

You cannot get a good education in a place which runs like a factory, with a hectic work pace, and never the chance for a relaxing physical diversion.

Therefore: Arrange sports facilities on campus, so that every point is within 400 to 500 feet of a place which is designed for sports and leisure a swimming pool, gym, sauna, tennis courts, etc.

Data in Pattern language

Local sports—basketball

27. CLASSROOM DISTRIBUTION

Have you ever tried to hold an intimate seminar for 10 students, in a huge classroom which has 70 or 80 seats?

Therefore: Construct classrooms in such a way that the total number of classrooms in any given sector of the university is proportional to the number of faculty offices in that sector, and so that the distribution of classrooms classified by number of seats, both in each sector and in the university as a whole, follows these percentages:

classroom type by number of seats	percentage of classrooms of this type
0–15	27 percent
16–30	35 percent
31–60	27 percent
61–90	4 percent
91–150	3 percent
151–300	3 percent
300 and up	1 percent

Data in Oregon files

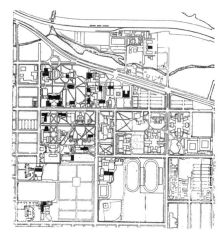

*Existing distribution of classrooms at
the University of Oregon*

*A distribution of classrooms
which follows the pattern*

28. DEPARTMENT HEARTH

When an academic department is just a collection of offices, without a focus, there is little chance for a sense of community to develop; and the possibility of an open exchange of ideas is diminished.

Therefore: For every department, create a social hearth. Place the hearth at the center of gravity of the department offices; and beside a path that everyone uses. Within the hearth, provide a lounge, department mail, coffee, supplies, small library, student information, etc. Make certain all department offices are within 500 feet of the hearth.

Data in Oregon files and in Pattern language under Common areas at the heart

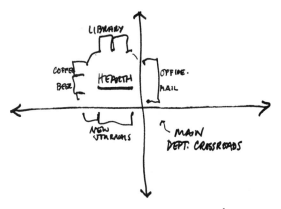

Department hearth at the crossroads

29. FACULTY STUDENT MIX

Students and faculty can benefit most from each other if they are able to develop mutual respect and common interests in a primary group. Learning and research cannot flourish without the sustained informal contacts which occur within such groups.

Therefore: Cluster student workplaces around faculty offices in groups of 5 to 10. Give each cluster a common entrance and a common area which contains seats, books, journals, hot plate, seminar table, and the like.

Data in Oregon files

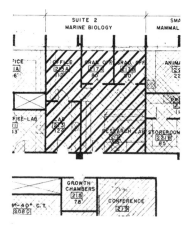

A faculty student cluster under construction in the biology labs at the University of Oregon

30. STUDENT WORKPLACE

There are not enough private workspaces for students at the university. The result is that students must study either in the student union or the library, or go home. Most go home for serious study; and this undermines the practical advantages of learning in a university community.

Therefore: Provide a private workspace on campus, for every student whose home is more than a five minute walk from campus; each workplace at least 25 square feet. Provide these places in departments, libraries, and student gathering places.

Data in Oregon files

Improvised student workspace

31. REAL LEARNING IN CAFES

Coffee shops, bookstores, films, and little restaurants are as vital to the process of education and personal growth as labs and exams. Without them the university is not a complete educational milieu.

Therefore: Encourage privately owned and managed shops, restaurants, cafes, theaters, etc., to locate on campus, on busy corners, so that they are accessible to both the campus population and the general public.

Data in Oregon files and Pattern language
under Street cafe

Cafe opposite Kings College, Cambridge

32. ARCADES

Arcades—covered walkways at the edge of buildings, which are partly inside the building, partly outside—play a vital role in the way that group territory and the society-at-large interact.

Therefore: Whenever paths pass beside buildings, create deep arcades over the paths, and open the group territory inside the building to these arcades. Gradually knit these arcades together until they form a covered system of paths throughout the community.

Data in Pattern language

Arcades connecting public life to buildings

135

This short list of summaries will give the reader some idea of the power and importance patterns can have, if they are used to guide development. We now discuss the practical steps which must be taken to promote the use of patterns, at the University of Oregon, and, above all, to make sure that the patterns are gradually improved and enlarged by members of the university community.

The important issues are these:

1. We want to make sure that the community can use the published pattern language.

2. We want to make sure that the patterns have the status of formally adopted planning and building principles.

3. We want to make sure that there is a mechanism by which new patterns can be introduced, and bad patterns replaced by better ones.

4. We want to make sure that there is a process which will guarantee the gradual improvement of patterns by empirical experiment and observations.

The practical procedures which we have used, at the University of Oregon, for maintaining these objectives, are captured by the following principle:

The principle of patterns: All design and construction will be guided by a collection of com-

munally adopted planning principles called patterns. To this end, the planning staff shall modify the published pattern language, by deleting and inserting patterns, to meet local needs; those patterns which have global impact on the community shall be adopted formally by the planning board, on behalf of the community; the collection of formally adopted patterns shall be reviewed annually at public hearings, where any member of the community can introduce new patterns, or revisions of old patterns, on the basis of explicitly stated observations and experiments.

The following details make this principle precise.

(i) *The planning staff shall modify the published pattern language by deleting and inserting patterns to meet local needs.*

In this task, it is essential to begin with a distinction between those patterns which are global and those which are detailed. The patterns we call global are the ones which have an overall impact on the community, and which can only be implemented at all when they are implemented piecemeal, by the joint effect of dozens, even hundreds, of different projects. They include patterns for open space, density, movement, etc. The patterns we call detailed, are those which can be implemented in a single building project. They include patterns for individual rooms, doors, windows, building construction and so on.

A Pattern Language contains both global and local patterns. In order to adapt this language to the needs of the community, we suggest that the global patterns be modified by the planning staff in the way we have described earlier in the chapter, and then presented to the planning board for formal adoption; and we suggest that the detailed patterns be modified much more informally, according to the initiative of the planning staff, in a series of detailed addenda to the published pattern language.

The global patterns which are formally adopted can be kept up-to-date in the files of the planning staff. They can then be issued, as a matter of course, to any users who initiate a project.

The detailed patterns do not need to be formally adopted. However, we suggest that the detailed patterns, with whatever modifications or addenda the planning staff have written, might also be given to every user design team when they begin a project, and to the architects who are hired later to detail the projects. It is possible to imagine, then, that every user design team, and every architect working on the completion of the users' projects, will work from some version—intact or modified—of the published pattern language, and will be able to use it to work out the smallest details of their buildings.

(ii) *Those patterns which have global impact on the community, shall be adopted formally by the planning board, on behalf of the community.*

Each pattern is a document, several pages long, complete with evidence, and arguments. Discussion of even a single pattern can be very time-consuming; discussion of thirty patterns all at once, in open session, would be almost impossible. It may, therefore, be helpful for the planning board to assign the task of evaluating the patterns to a subcommittee, and only debate with the full board those points which are in doubt.

This is the procedure which has been followed in Oregon. The thirty-two patterns presented in the foregoing summaries have been adopted by the board on the recommendation of a subcommittee which examined them in detail.

(iii) *The collection of formally adopted patterns shall be reviewed annually at public hearings, where any member of the community can introduce new patterns, or change old ones.*

The planning board has agreed to review the patterns, formally, once a year. At this review members of the campus community can introduce new patterns; and old patterns may be changed or dropped when experience shows them to be wrong.

To illustrate this process, we shall describe one example case where a user group studied a new pattern for child care, and then proposed it formally to the planning board for inclusion in the list of adopted patterns.

Michael Shellenbarger and Pamela Gauld, two faculty members from the School of Architecture, and several students, surveyed the existing child care facilities. They found that they were not adequate; there were far more young families with parents working and taking classes, than these centers could serve. They also discovered that many faculty and students believed the university would benefit from the presence of children if the child-care centers could be properly integrated.

The group drew up their conclusions in the form of a series of campus child care patterns. The patterns propose a series of child care home bases, across the campus, each one for 20 to 30 children; and with each center containing an outdoor play area overlapping with the routine outdoor life of the campus: with sitting walls and tables just at the edge, to form a meeting ground for the children and the community.

These patterns have been proposed to the university. Shellenbarger and Gauld are asking that they be adopted as part of the governing set of campus patterns. At this writing, the proposal is before the Planning Board and will be debated and voted upon at the next session on new patterns.

(iv) *The board shall only accept new patterns, or revisions of old patterns, on the basis of explicitly stated observations and experiments.*

The patterns stand or fall according to their ability to solve the problem to which they are addressed. Since our understanding of these problems is always rough, and the problems themselves may change, it is essential that the set of patterns be continually improved. This happens naturally when the community understands the tentative nature of patterns, and takes an openminded, experimental attitude toward them. To encourage this, the planning staff has begun to describe simple critical experiments for each pattern. Once these experiments are made public, they invite people to test the patterns, and improve them.

Here are two examples. The pattern, *Living learning circle* says that some student housing should be built in and among the academic buildings. Is it true that students want to live on campus? If so, about how many? And what are the circumstances that make this kind of living desirable? Pilot experiments were set up to answer these questions. A group of students worked on the experiments, and collected and interpreted the data. They discovered that about 25 percent of the student body want to live on campus. This is less than we expected. But they also discovered that those who do want to live on campus, when presented with four different possible locations for the housing, do most often choose the housing which is mixed in with departments.

Another example—*Classroom distribution*. This pattern began with the rather obvious idea that meeting rooms, classrooms, and lecture halls should match the actual distribution of group meetings in the community. A straightforward investigation was set up: Classify all the academic meetings that take place on campus, according to the size of the group: What is their statistical distribution? This investigation was tackled by Hal Napper, a member of the campus planning staff.

Napper found, surprisingly, that the great majority of classes held had groups of 5, 10, perhaps 20 people, while the majority of classrooms being built were for groups of 30 to 150 people. This simple finding completely transforms the existing building program and gives tremendous strength to the pattern: Build the majority of classrooms and labs to accommodate small intimate seminars; build the larger rooms and the lecture halls more gradually, only when there is a clearcut need.

We propose that the planning board invite students and faculty members to set up critical experiments for the adopted patterns, and to make these experiments public. This activity can be encouraged as unit work, thesis work, etc. The record of experiments for each pattern can be kept on open file and published in the newspaper. Gradually, then, each pattern can be subjected to a cycle of pilot study, experiment, and revision at the hands of the community.

CHAPTER 5

DIAGNOSIS

We now come back to the original objectives of a master plan. A master plan is intended to create global order. It tries to do this by making a map of the future. We have shown that this procedure has fatal flaws; and we have proposed to replace the master plan with a process of piecemeal growth, in which individual building increments are designed by their users.

But we have not yet solved the problem which the master plan was intended to solve. It is still not clear where global order will come from, without a master plan.

This problem has been described in theory in *The Timeless Way of Building*. It is explained there that the thousands of small acts of building can be made to create larger, global, order if each pattern that is built is always built in such a way as to contribute to some larger pattern as well. In this chapter we shall focus on the kind of practical device which is needed to make this abstract process happen in reality.

Let us assume that there is widespread participation by faculty, students, and staff in the process of design, as we have recommended in Chapter 2. And let us assume that the university can finance a large number of small projects every year, according to the principle of piecemeal growth described in Chapter 3. Finally, let us assume that the community has adopted the fifty-five patterns listed in Chapter 4 as guidelines for their designs.

What will be the combined effect of these actions on the university environment? Will they help to create a great university over the next twenty years? Or will they create chaos? How can we be sure that hundreds of piecemeal design acts will gradually create global order throughout the community?

To make this problem as concrete as possible, here are four examples of cases where a piecemeal planning process, in which users propose projects more or less at random, would probably break down.

1. The Willamette River runs through the University of Oregon, but people cannot get to it. They are cut off from the riverbank by a highway,

a railroad track, and a fence. Some kind of development is required to remedy this situation, but it is a complicated project, covering many acres. Suppose no user group expresses interest. Does this mean that the riverfront will remain inaccessible for years?

2. Suppose that the bike paths which run through the university are almost complete, but the system as a whole is missing a crucial link. Who will create this link? What if no one comes forward to take up this project?

3. It is possible to infer, from the patterns, that the University of Oregon should grow toward the northwest. But the argument which leads to this conclusion is complex; and it is unlikely that individual project teams will happen to make this inference for themselves. How then can this inference be recorded, once it is made? And how can it be communicated to users?

4. Our experience with the patterns has led us to believe that the best way of integrating the patterns *University streets, Accessible greens, Building complex, Activity nodes, Wings of light* and *Positive outdoor space* is to create a system of small buildings along narrow pedestrian streets, the streets meeting in activity nodes and surrounding

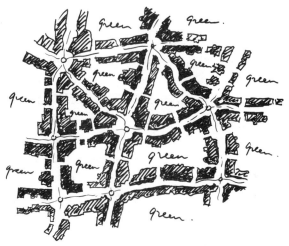

The sort of overall structure these six patterns
generate together

larger greens. A group of users who have not had
the benefit of our experience may not be able to
synthesize these six patterns quite so easily. How
can our experience be recorded and made available
to the people who need it?

These examples make it clear that a piecemeal
planning process, with designs made by users, could
easily fail to generate the global order which the
university environment needs. In this chapter we
shall present a way of solving this problem.

We propose to solve the problem in a way that
is almost perfectly analogous to the way in which

it is solved in nature. We therefore begin by explaining the problem, and its solution, for an organism. *When an organism grows, how is it that the millions of different cells that are growing at various places throughout the organism manage to form a unified whole, with as much order in the overall structure of the organism, as in the small parts which make it up?* This question—perhaps the deepest and most important question of biology —is illuminating for the following reason. Here again, we have a process of piecemeal growth. It is clear that somehow an organism manages to guide the piecemeal process in such a way as to create a unified whole. But it is also clear that the way this happens is not at all like master planning. There is certainly no huge blueprint, with billions of slots, which fixes the exact position of every last cell according to some pre-ordained plan. Yet, somehow the organism grows as a whole, under the impetus of piecemeal processes.

How is the problem solved in an organism? Essentially, the problem is solved by a process of diagnosis and local repair.

The organism, from the very beginnings of its life, is constantly monitoring its own internal state. In particular, those parts of the organism where critical variables have gone beyond their allowable limits are identified. We may call this the diagnosis. In response to the diagnosis, the organism sets in motion growth processes to repair this situation. It is fairly certain that the broad framework of this growth is governed by the endocrine system, which creates a variety of chemical fields throughout the organism. These fields are created by changing concentrations of various hormones; and together these fields guide detailed growth, at the cellular level. These are the *growth fields.*

The growth fields act chemically to encourage growth in certain parts of the organism and to inhibit growth in others. At those places where growth occurs, the cells multiply. The detailed configuration of the cells which grow at these places is governed mainly by the genetic code, carried by every cell. This controls the exact development of the cells, and the arrangement of their growth, splitting, change and decay. In fine detail, this process is controlled by the interaction of the genetic code with the chemistry of the growth fields in which the cells are growing. This guarantees that local configurations of cells are not only intrinsically suitable but are also properly integrated with the whole.

We see, then, that global order within the organism is governed at two levels. First, the growth fields create the context for growth, and determine the location where growth shall occur. Then the genetic code carried by the cells controls the local configurations which grow at those locations, modified always by interaction with the growth fields themselves.

This process not only repairs the mature organism, when it is damaged, or diseased; it is also responsible for guiding the embryo during its earliest growth. It is thus responsible for shaping the mature organism, not only for repairing and maintaining it when it is finally complete. In short, the original global form of the organism comes from the very same process of diagnosis and repair which keeps it stable once it is mature.

We propose to solve the problem of global order in the university by means of a very similar process of diagnosis and repair. Let us look at this process in detail. The various parts of the university environment are successful to the extent that they solve the problems that recur within them. For example, a department is successful to the extent that it solves the problems of human scale, common meeting ground, and comfortable work space. If it feels too large, if there is no central hearth, and if the classrooms and offices are unpleasant, the department will never be a living entity. These facts are given by the patterns. When *Department of 400*, *Department hearth*, and *Faculty student mix* are present in a university department, its environment is more successful than when they are missing.

Once a set of patterns have been adopted by the university, it is therefore possible to look at the environment and mark the places where the patterns have broken down. Since we can tell where each pattern is present, and where it is missing, we can diagnose the whole university environment, pattern by pattern. We may sketch the diagnosis for each pattern in the form of a map which has four colors: yellow, orange, red, and red hatching—summarizing the "state of that pattern" in the environment. Yellow indicates places where the pattern exists, and where the problem in question is solved—places to be left intact. Orange indicates places where the pattern very nearly exists, but where some repair is required. Red refers to those areas which are virtually unusable, even though some version of the pattern exists. Such areas are marked for radical repair. And finally, red hatching refers to those areas where the pattern does not exist at all, so that the problem will remain unsolved until the pattern gets created there.

Here is an example of the diagnostic map for the pattern, *Positive outdoor space*.

Diagnosis of Positive outdoor space

The areas marked yellow represent outdoor spaces that are good positive spaces; they have the right amount of enclosure and the right amount of openness; and the problem discussed in the pattern is solved. These areas should be left exactly as they are. The orange areas represent outdoor spaces that require some modification, before they completely meet the pattern. They are perhaps not enclosed enough, or they are too enclosed. But they are in good enough shape so that trees, hedges, walls or buildings, carefully placed, can create the pattern perfectly. The solid red areas are open spaces which are in need of more drastic repair. They are not used at all because of a serious problem of location, access or some other problem which calls for complete reworking of the place; they can be considered for some other use entirely. The red hatched areas indicate areas of the campus where the problem stated in the pattern is felt, and the solution is completely missing—these areas have no positive open spaces at all.

This map, then, with its supplementary statements defines a crude growth field for *Positive outdoor space.* If the yellow areas are left intact, the orange areas slightly improved, the red areas drastically re-built, and the red-hatched areas given altogether new positive outdoor spaces, then gradually the pattern *Positive outdoor space* will be repaired, and grow, until it governs all the out-door spaces in the university. Just so, a collection of all 55 diagnostic maps, for all 55 patterns, will establish overall growth fields for the entire university environment.

By themselves, however, these maps are not enough. To establish the health of the environment as a whole, we need a composite map, summarizing the 55 pattern-maps. Such a map contains everything we know about the state of the environment; and users can scan it easily to pick out the information that is relevant to their projects. Let us look at one corner of this composite diagnosis for the University of Oregon.

Like the monitoring process in organisms, this composite map can guide the growth and repair of the environment. It tells us which places are in relatively good health—for example, the open space in the center is marked yellow because it works well today, and should therefore be left alone. The map tells us which places require simple modification—for example, the potential university street, running north-south between the buildings, is marked orange, to show that it needs minor modifications to make it into a properly functioning "university street." The map tells us which

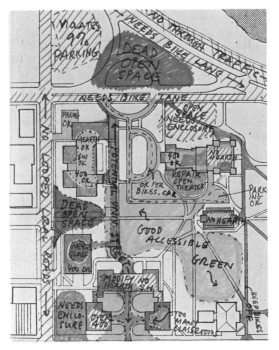

*Section of the University of Oregon,
diagnosis—Northwest corner*

areas are dead and unusable—the triangular open
space to the north between the two main roads is
marked red because it does not work at all. And the
map tells us where patterns are required—for example, the red hatched roads need bike lanes. In
short, the map establishes an overall growth field
for the university community.

There is one important point to be made about the creation of the composite diagnosis: It cannot be derived entirely from the maps of the individual patterns. The pattern-maps are always incomplete and, at best, give only an approximate analysis of what is healthy and what is sick in the environment. If we try to derive the composite map strictly from the pattern-maps, we shall find that some insights for repairing the environment are "lost." These insights may range from the obvious to the profound. We know, for example, that the theater building is poorly ventilated; the studios are unusable in the summer and need air-conditioning. But we do not have an adopted pattern on the proper context for air-conditioning. If we stick to the pattern maps, we lose this piece of information. Or consider an open space, which seems to contain all the patterns but still feels cold and dead. We know that it needs something, but we are not sure just what. Again, if we stick only to the pattern maps we will lose this feeling.

It is not simply a question of writing patterns to cover these insights—though that is helpful and should be done. The fact is that there will always be such insights: *our feelings for the life of the environment will always outstrip the current set*

of patterns. And we must be free to add these intuitions to the diagnostic map.

Superficially, the diagnosis may seem like a conventional master plan. There is, however, a great
difference. The master plan tells us what is right,
for the future. The diagnosis tells us what is
wrong, now, in the present. The diagnosis, and a
typical master plan, are also very different in the
amount of detail they portray. The master plan,
since it is intended to show positive action, shows
rather little detail—only broad outlines of what
ought to be done in any given area. The diagnosis,
since it shows only what is wrong, can go into
enormous detail in pinpointing errors: a seat which
is in shade, flowers which are being trampled, walls
blocking a necessary view, a room which is too
small, a path which does not have the light it
needs—all these can be shown on the diagnosis, in
great detail. And yet, with all this detail the diagnosis leaves the people who are making up designs for new buildings far freer than the master
plan, because it fires their imagination, challenges
them to invent ways of changing things to repair
all the detailed defects of the present.

Finally, a historical note. We have discovered
that a process very similar to the idea of diagnosis

played a basic role in the creation of global order in the free city-states of medieval Italy. John Larner, in *Culture and Society in Italy 1290–1420* (Charles Scribner's Sons, New York, 1971), points out that the organic character of these towns was not the result of some haphazard "instinctive sense of form-correlation." Instead the towns emerged from a very definite planning process. The process was built around the existence of "decrees" and "laws," similar to our patterns, and a yearly review of the town by a citizens' group, a process similar to our diagnosis. It was the responsibility of this citizens' group to devise incremental projects, in the spirit of the "decrees."

In Siena the Statutes of the Road Supervisors, drawn up in 1290, consisted of about 300 decrees concerned with urban development. In these it was laid down that at the beginning of May each year a committee, responsible to the General Council, should survey the town in each of its administrative divisions. Then, in the first or second week of the month, it was to draw up building plans for the next year. For example, on 10 May 1297 this committee sponsored no less than 18 laws. Of these, three provided for work on the Cathedral, two treated of the condition of private palaces around the central square, two referred to arches across streets, four dealt with well-building and lavatories, and seven with plans for the widening and paving of streets. In addition it asked for an annual budget of £4,000 to be assigned to the building of the Palace of the Commune, discussed plans for a new Baptistery, and inaugurated a new committee to supervise water and wells. . . . Normally, the men who served on these committees were not building specialists but ordinary citizens. Dante served on the Florentine committee, and during his term of office took part in making arrangements for widening via San Procolo.

The practical steps which must be taken to make sure that the university maintains an annual diagnosis as the central part of its planning process are given by the following principle:

The principle of diagnosis: The well being of the whole will be protected by an annual diagnosis which explains, in detail, which spaces are alive and which ones dead, at any given moment in the history of the community. To this end, the planning staff, working together with the people who use individual spaces, shall prepare an annual diagnostic map for the entire community; this map shall be formally adopted by the planning board, after a series of public hearings, and then published and made available to everyone who wants to initiate a project.

The following details make this principle precise:

(i) *The planning staff, working together with the people who use individual spaces, shall prepare an annual diagnostic map for the entire community.*

We propose that the campus planning staff take responsibility for the annual diagnosis of the campus. This diagnosis should take the form of a single large map (possibly in segments), supplemented by separate maps for each formally adopted pattern. The diagnosis will be most accurate if the staff makes the diagnosis with help from the established user groups in each neighborhood of the campus. They may even farm out the development of some part of the map to interested groups. The staff, however, should have final responsibility for preparing the diagnosis.

In the first year, the whole diagnosis will have to be made from scratch. In later years, large parts of last year's diagnosis will still be valid, so the diagnosis can be made by modifying and updating last year's maps.

(ii) *This map shall be formally adopted by the planning board, after a series of public hearings, and then published and made available to everyone who wants to initiate a project.*

The annual diagnosis is presented by the planning staff, to the planning board, and is then adopted formally, after discussion and revision. Since adoption of the diagnosis is so important for each year's building schedule, this meeting should include a public hearing, well advertised, where any members of the community may propose amendments to the diagnostic maps.

The adopted diagnosis will work best for the community, if it is formally published, reprinted in the community newspaper, and posted in public places, so that every member of the university community is likely to see it during the course of normal business on campus. With the diagnosis constantly in front of them, there is a good chance that people will pay more attention to their environment, see what is not working properly, and invent projects to repair the defects.

CHAPTER 6

COORDINATION

We are now ready to imagine the emergence of organic order at the University of Oregon over the next twenty or thirty years. As the title of this chapter indicates, it hinges on a process of coordination which uses the mechanism of the centralized budget to make sure that the projects which get built are always the ones which contribute most to the emergence of organic order in the community —and it hinges on the fact that this process is so clear, and so public, that it acts as an incentive which encourages groups of users to propose projects which are good for the community in this larger, coordinative sense.

However, we must repeat, emphatically, what we have already said in the introduction: namely, that the process of coordination through a centralized budget is not the proper way to create organic order in a community. Very bluntly put, any centralized budget will inevitably have totalitarian elements in it. The point is made over and over again in our other books that a truly organic order will only grow up under conditions where individual acts are free, and coordinated by mutual responsibility, not by constraint or control.

We believe, in short, that the full-fledged organic order which we seek can only be created by a form of responsible anarchy, in which people are free to build as they please, are strongly encouraged by self-interest to act on behalf of larger community needs, but are not forced to do so by centralized fiscal or legal control.

Obviously, this form of society cannot exist in any community where there is a centralized budget. The process which we now describe is therefore the rather inadequate best which can be achieved under the non-ideal conditions of a centralized budget.

With this warning, we are now ready to state the principle of coordination.

The principle of coordination: Finally, the slow emergence of organic order in the whole will be assured by a funding process which regulates the stream of individual projects put forward by users. To this end, every project which seeks funds for construction shall be submitted to the planning board, on a standard form, which explains its relation to the currently adopted patterns and diagnosis; the projects submitted for funding in any given budget year shall be put in order of priority for funds by the planning board, acting in open session; at this session projects shall be judged by the extent to which they conform to the community's adopted patterns and diagnosis—with the clear understanding that projects will be built in every size range, and that projects of different size will not compete for funds.

We shall first describe the details which make this principle precise, and shall then end the chapter, and the book, with examples which show, in practice, how this principle leads to the emergence of organic order in the university community.

(i) *Every project which seeks funds for construction shall be submitted to the planning board on a standard form, which explains its relation to the currently adopted patterns and diagnosis.*

To submit a project to the university, the members of every user group must fill out the following standard form on which they show the design of the proposed project, its cost, its expected source of funds, and the conformity or non-conformity

to all formally adopted patterns and diagnosis.
This procedure must be followed for all projects,
regardless of their cost or source of funding.

The University
Planning Board

University of Oregon
Eugene, Oregon

PROJECT APPLICATION
Title Sheet

PROJECT TITLE:

USER GROUP (Give the name of the project team, the names and
affiliations of its individual members, and the user population
they represent):

DATE:

Present your project proposal on no more than five pages, attached
to this title sheet, and arrange the description of your project
under the following headings:

1. BASIC PROBLEM: What is the basic problem that the group is
trying to solve?

2. PROPOSAL: Give an overall description of the proposed project: Where is it to be located? What is its character with
respect to repair, new growth? How is it related to the
surrounding area? Enclose a drawing which summarizes the
proposal.

3. PATTERNS: Show the evolution of the project and its relation
to the university's adopted patterns.

4. DIAGNOSIS: How has the project responded to the current diagnostic maps; specifically how have the surrounding areas been
improved?

5. COSTS: What is the estimated cost of the project?

6. FUNDING: What is the proposed source of funds?

The application form for projects

165

Even though this procedure has slightly bureaucratic overtones, we consider it essential that every project, no matter what its type, be submitted for approval, and for funding, on the same form, so that the members of the planning board can test different projects against the criteria given by patterns and by the current diagnosis; and can then compare them equally with one another.

We stress the fact that every single construction or planning project, no matter what its source of funds, must be put on a form of this kind, and must then pass through the planning board, before it gets approval or funds. For example, projects which concern routine maintenance, or modifications in the student dormitories—which might at present bypass the normal planning process, because physical plant and housing have their own budgets, and do not require funds from the state *must also be presented on these forms*. New allocations of space, and rehabilitation of existing space *must, in just the same way, be presented on these forms*.

At present, at the University of Oregon, a great many of the "minor" projects in the university do not go through the campus planning committee —because they rely on internal funds administered by maintenance, or housing funds, or other special funds. But, as we have stressed, especially in the chapters on piecemeal growth and diagnosis, it is just the multitude of these small, local projects which help most to create organic order in the community. If these small projects fail to make the contribution they can make to the environment as a whole, as defined by the adopted global patterns, then there is very little chance that the remaining larger projects will, by themselves, be able to create organic order.

(ii) *The projects submitted for funding in any given budget year shall be put in order of priority for funds by the planning board, in open session.*

In a given budget period, the planning board shall gather together all the proposed projects on the forms described above, and assign to them a priority for funding. The deadline for submitting proposals and the date of the funding session must be well-publicized. We imagine that the board would work *in camera* to prepare a tentative order of priority, and would then present this tentative order at an open session where proponents and opponents of the various projects could challenge the tentative order of priority. Finally, after debate and challenges, the board would make their final order while still in open session.

(iii) *At this session projects shall be judged by the extent to which they conform to the community's adopted patterns and diagnosis—with the clear understanding that projects will be built in every size range, and that projects of different size will not compete for funds.*

The criteria for judging the projects are the community's pattern language, and the current diagnostic map. In effect, the board is charged with assigning priority to those projects which both embody the adopted patterns, and help to repair the defects discovered by the diagnostic process. Again, since the fine points of such matters are open to interpretation and subtleties of judgment, we imagine that these sessions are open, so that the public can hear the debate, make their own case, and show their approval or disapproval of the board's decisions.

Of course, the projects must be judged in a way that is consonant with the principle of piecemeal growth. To this end, we propose that projects be compared only against those which are in their own size range. That is, there will be *several* priority lists, one for each budget category; a given proposal will only compete for funds against other proposals in its category; and it is understood that some projects from each category will be funded every year.

One of these priority lists—the one dealing with the smallest category (less than $1000)—might have to be constructed more than once a year, in order to make sure that people could get on with small projects while their enthusiasm lasts—and the board would have to agree to review projects for this list very quickly indeed, since there will be many of them, and it will be impossible to review them all in great detail. This would mean, for example, that a member of the faculty who decided to renovate his office—to open up a wall to the outdoors, and build a deck or balcony, to furnish this area for small seminars, and landscape it, all for $500—could get his money with a minimum of procedural difficulty. Certainly, if such tiny projects are subject to formal, yearly review, they will be robbed of their spontaneity—the very quality that makes them worthwhile.

The principle of coordination is the last of the six principles we propose. In a way, this sixth principle summarizes the other five principles and gives the final details of administration required to grow an organic environment. We shall now illustrate the action of the six principles, with examples. First we shall show a single project; then we shall simulate the effect of hundreds of individual projects, growing together over the next thirty years. As we shall see, the cooperative action of hundreds of projects, guided by the six principles, over the years, will guarantee, almost inevitably, that the university community grows, slowly, toward a state of greater and greater wholeness.

To illustrate a single project we have chosen a building for administrative services. Administrative services are now, at the time of writing, concentrated almost entirely in an old wooden building—Emerald Hall. The building is run down, it has not been cared for; parts of it are beyond repair. There is a shortage of space: some of the services are too cramped to function adequately. In addition, many important adjacency requirements are not now being met: individual services are poorly related to each other, and many are poorly related to the parts of the community they serve. On the whole, there is strong sentiment in the university community that the administrative services need a new building of some kind.

Let us imagine that the administrative staff creates a project team to initiate the project.

The project team's task is to develop a rudimentary proposal for an administrative services building, which they can present to the University Planning Board. The first step is to review the existing situation in detail, to survey the building, and the current diagnostic maps. The outcome of this review is a building program: a description of the amount of space required, the kinds of spaces proposed, as well as an indication of which parts of the existing buildings are to be preserved and renovated and which parts are to be rebuilt.

Using the program as a point of reference, the team then builds up a design. The patterns are taken one by one, and are applied to the site; the design evolves gradually, with the help of the Planning Staff; the team makes a sequence of sketches to record their design decisions. The final drawing—the schematic design—includes a plan for repair and improvements to the old building and grounds, and a plan for new construction. This proposal is then presented to the planning board.

To make the proposal comparable to other projects of the same scale, and to insure that the adopted patterns and diagnostic maps are taken seriously, they must submit the proposal on the standard form described above.

The University
Planning Board

University of Oregon
Eugene, Oregon

PROJECT APPLICATION
Title Sheet

PROJECT TITLE: Administrative Services Building

USER GROUP (Give the name of the project team, the names and
affiliations of its individual members, and the user population
they represent): We are a project team of seven persons: Joe
Smith, etc...five drawn from the administrative staff, one
student, and one member of the Campus Planning Office. As
the project proceeds to the more detailed stages of the design, we shall split up the work among the relevant
interest groups.

DATE: May 10, 1971

Present your project proposal on no more than five pages, attached
to this title sheet, and arrange the description of your project
under the following headings:

1. BASIC PROBLEM: What is the basic problem that the group is
   trying to solve?

2. PROPOSAL: Give an overall description of the proposed project: Where is it to be located? What is its character with
   respect to repair, new growth? How is it related to the
   surrounding area? Enclose a drawing which summarizes the
   proposal.

3. PATTERNS: Show the evolution of the project and its relation
   to the university's adopted patterns.

4. DIAGNOSIS: How has the project responded to the current diagnostic maps; specifically how have the surrounding areas been
   improved?

5. COSTS: What is the estimated cost of the project?

6. FUNDING: What is the proposed source of funds?

Here is a simulated version of this form, as if it
had been filled out by the user group for the administrative services project.

COORDINATION

1. BASIC PROBLEM: Three basic problems led us to initiate this project:

    A. Repair of existing facilities: The current facilities are badly in need of repair; approximately half of the Emerald complex has been assessed as "not worth repairing" by the University Architect; and new construction will be required to replace it.

    B. Organization of existing facilities: Services with critical mutual needs are not properly organized; and the services that deal directly with the community are remote from the everyday life of the community.

    C. Growth: The services are currently operating with a shortage of space - based on entitlement figures. Thus, in addition to repair, replacement and reorganization of spaces, the project includes plans for new growth.

2. PROPOSAL: We propose a rennovation of the south half of Emerald Hall, and the replacement of the north half with new buildings. The new buildings can be built in three stages, as a collection of small buildings, running east-west along 13th Street, between Erb and Emerald. The buildings are connected at the second level by arcades. At the ground level along the street, the community services form "shop fronts". The buildings open, behind the street, to open space - a green to the south and a plaza to the north. At the west end of the street they form a small square with the Science Annex and the Student Union. The following drawing summarizes our proposal:

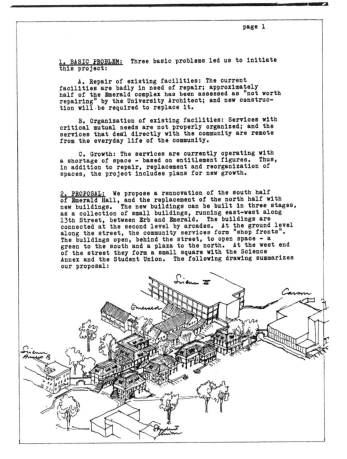

COORDINATION

3. PATTERNS: The following patterns played the strongest
role in shaping our proposal: University Streets, Activity
Nodes, Human Buildings, Small Services Without Red Tape,
Small Student Unions, Tiny Parking Lots, Circulation
Realms and Arcades.

The following sequence of diagrams, shows the evolution
of our design, and pinpoints the patterns, as they affected
the design.

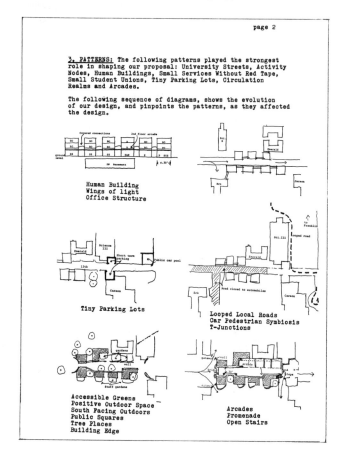

Human Building
Wings of light
Office Structure

Tiny Parking Lots

Looped Local Roads
Car Pedestrian Symbiosis
T-Junctions

Accessible Greens
Positive Outdoor Space
South Facing Outdoors
Public Squares
Tree Places
Building Edge

Arcades
Promenade
Open Stairs

COORDINATION

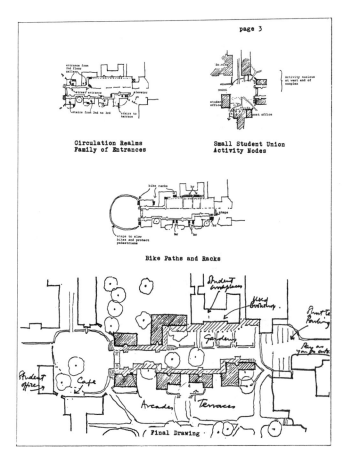

**Circulation Realms
Family of Entrances**

**Small Student Union
Activity Nodes**

Bike Paths and Racks

Final Drawing

175

COORDINATION

4. DIAGNOSIS: With respect to the current set of diagnostic maps, our proposal improves the area in the
following ways: We have established an extension of
the university street, called for along 13th Street;
we have helped to complete the local green - Carson
Quad, and the Science Plaza; we have created a small
square adjacent to the student union, a gathering place
for the area; and we have included in the plans for the
repair of the old Emerald Building, 2,000 square feet
of student workspace, and space for a small student
operated book exchange.

We have failed to include in our design several patterns
which the Board may feel are pertinent: Living Learning
Circle (i.e. student housing); 9% Parking; and on the
north side of the street, South Facing Outdoors.

Living Learning Circle: The project is already straining
the limits of piecemeal growth, and we shall have to build
it in several stages. Furthermore, with Carson Dorm near-
by, and still partially used for student housing, we believe this part of the University already contains a
sufficient mix of housing.

9% Parking: We have not removed any parking from the area,
and we have created two small lots to the east. Until
the parking commission establishes the zones of parking
responsibility in each sector of the campus, we think it
is incorrect for a project of this scale to include a
major parking plan.

South Facing Outdoors: Only the north buildings violate
this pattern. However, because these buildings are
helping to define and improve the character of the
Science Quad, and since their south edges have been developed as useful places, we feel the plan is justified.

5. COSTS: The entire project, as it is now conceived,
provides 59,200 gross square feet of space; approximate
cost of the project, including repairs to Emerald Hall,
would be $1,600,000.

6. FUNDING: We propose that this money be granted from
the General Fund.

Next we present a simulation of the entire University of Oregon community, growing over a period of thirty years. The simulation shows the accumulation of hundreds of projects, some at the scale of the administrative services project, a few slightly larger, most smaller in scale. All the projects are roughly compatible with the patterns and the diagnosis that might emerge during these years.

Of course these drawings are *not* intended to represent a specific plan for the University of Oregon. As we have said over and over again, we want at all costs to prevent the construction of any map of the future which claims "This is how the university ought to be organized in the year 2000."

It is impossible to predict how the university will grow because the growth process is guided by patterns and diagnostic maps which themselves change constantly to match new conditions and the new interpretations of different design teams and different planning boards.

Trying to establish an exact picture of the university environment in the year 2000 is rather like trying to give an exact picture of an oak tree—the lay of its branches, the exact width and shape of its trunk, in advance, as the acorn begins to sprout. It cannot be done. The best we could do would be to look at mature oak trees that have grown under similar conditions. From these trees we could gather a feeling, but not an exact picture, for what our tree will eventually be like. That is what we are trying to do for the University of Oregon, in the sketches which follow.

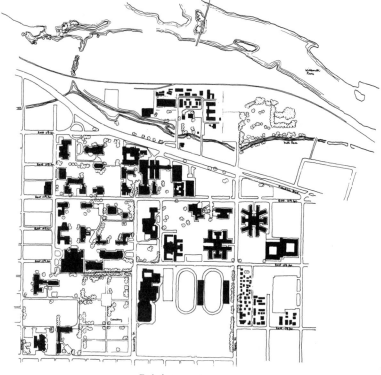

Existing campus

(Note: The amount of development we have shown is based on estimates from the University's Office of Planning and Institutional Research. For each decade the drawings show a growth of approximately 800,000 gross indoor square feet. These figures are based on a slight increase in the current enrollment.)

Growth during the 1970's. Here we imagine that Franklin Boulevard has been moved over toward the railroad, to bring the entire campus into one local transport area. We see the beginning of a promenade being formed at 13th Avenue, and university streets at the southwest corner of campus and in the dorm area to the west. Outdoor spaces start being better defined as new projects are built. Parts of the dorms are renovated for academic uses, and a student community is developed by the river. A garage with shops along the street is built for commuters at the northwest corner of campus, and the parking lots on campus are made smaller and equipped with meters for short-term parking use.

Growth during the 1980's. Here we show a continuation of the trends begun during the 70's: The development of 13th Avenue as a promenade is emphasized further and the university streets are strengthened. More fingers of university development reach into the town, and more privately run shops and cafes locate themselves on university streets within the campus. Another student community is built by the river which, together with

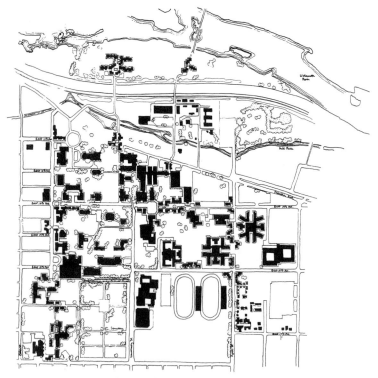

Growth during the 1970's

the old one, forms a large enough neighborhood for the addition of a small school. More outdoor spaces are improved as additional classrooms, offices, and student housing projects are added; another parking structure with street shops is built on the northeast corner of campus.

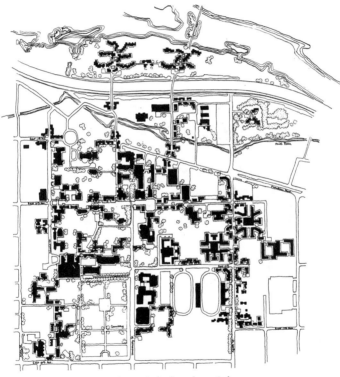

Growth during the 1980's

Growth during the 1990's. Here we show the campus as it might mature toward the end of the century. Arcades now form an almost continuous system, as do the bike paths. The campus is completely free of through traffic. Additional research, office, and classroom spaces have been added. A

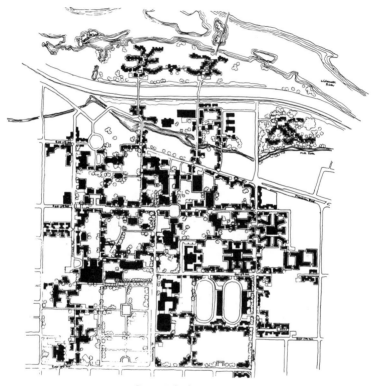

Growth during the 1990's

third student community is built near the millrace.
The promenade on 13th Avenue and the other
university streets are highly developed. Outdoor
rooms, gateways, and arcades complete many of
the open spaces.

In the sequence of these three drawings we see
how organic order slowly does emerge. Certain
morphological features appear and reappear—the
university streets opening into greens, the town
penetrating the university, the small two- and
three-story buildings with many public entrances
and the connecting arcades, the scattered centers
of sports and informal gatherings. Yet these features, though recurrent, always occur in new forms
and variations: each corner of the community has
a character of its own, each green and each building is unique. The variety is infinite but ordered. It
is certainly not the order of the master plan: the
growth has not been fixed in advance; development does not follow a pre-cooked outline; there
is a great deal of immediate responsiveness between
the various parts.

Finally, to make it abundantly clear that it is
the process itself which leads to organic order, not
any one fixed plan, we shall examine one part of
the drawing and see how its details might change

because of local circumstances, and how the effects
of this one change might then ripple out and effect
a whole area.

Consider the project for administrative services,
which we gave as an example earlier in this chapter. This project appears in the first large simulation, as one of the imaginary projects built in the
1970's. The buildings that follow, over the thirty
years, respond to its presence.

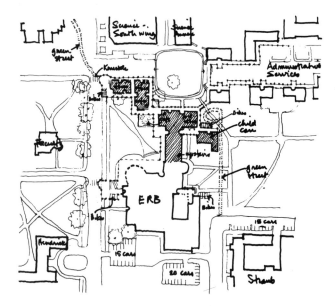

*Growth responding to the administrative
services project*

The extension of the student union creates a gathering place at the mouth of the "administration street," the child care building helps to form a court with the "back" of one of the service buildings, and both buildings help to define a large green to the east. Once the administration buildings are set down, the later projects respond to it, and help to improve the places which it creates around it.

But suppose the administrative project was never built. How would the student union, or the child care, or the greens develop then? Certainly they would have to be quite different, for they would then have to adapt to an entirely different whole— a whole that did not include the administrative project, and whose diagnostic maps were therefore different.

Specifically, let us imagine that the project for the repair and extension of the student union came into being *before* the administrative project. In this case the new union buildings are free to respond to the potential gathering place to the west of the existing union, and to develop the north-south road into a university street and leave the east-west road intact. In the absence of the administration project, this design responds to dif-

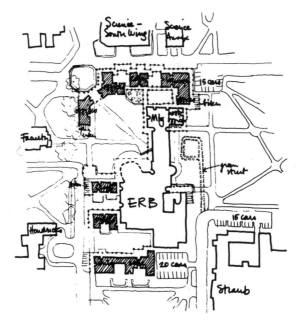

*Growth in the absence of the administrative
services project*

ferent features in the existing landscape and therefore takes on an entirely different shape.

And once this project is set down, the next development must respond to *it:* continuing to develop the university street, leaving the east-west
road for access, etc. The effects ripple out, and over
the years this simple change in timing leads to a
local environment whose form is entirely different
in detail from the form of that area in the simula-

tion we have shown—even though it is still a product of the same general morphology.

Our point is now transparent. The precise order that emerges as a result of the gradual coordination of hundreds of acts of piecemeal design cannot be known in advance; it can only arise slowly out of a community that is sharing patterns, responding to diagnosis and taking responsibility for its own plans and designs.

A precise plan for the University of Oregon cannot be fixed in advance. If it is to be an open, organic plan, it must grow from the hands of the community itself.

ACKNOWLEDGMENTS

As always, we have been helped immensely in this work by our friends. We wish to thank the people of the University of Oregon for their help during our visits to the campus: President Clark gave us much needed support. Al Urqhart, Dick Gale, and the members of the Campus Planning Committee reviewed the work at various stages and made many contributions. Ray Hawk and John Lallas helped us coordinate the work with existing campus policy; and Jack Hunderup provided the critical dialogue which led to the development of the diagnostic maps discussed in Chapter 5.

Dean Trotter, John McManus, Royce Salzman, and Dick Benedum, from the School of Music, worked with us on the design project presented in Chapter 2. Jerry Finrow, and many of his students in the School of Architecture, helped us with the experiments required to develop the patterns in Chapter 4.

ACKNOWLEDGMENTS

Our friends at the Center, Max, Ingrid, Meg, Mary Louise, and Priscilla gave us support and encouragement throughout the job. Ib Borring, visiting from Denmark, stayed and worked with us steadily during the first six months of the job; he contributed a great deal—especially to the development of the patterns. And we should like to thank the staff of the Campus Planning Office— Hal Napper and Banks Upshaw for their help, and Harry Van Oudenallen, the new Campus Planner, for his enthusiasm in following through with the implementation of the planning process.

And finally we extend our very special and warm thanks to Larry Bissett, who was Campus Planner when we did the bulk of the work, and to Bob Harris, the Dean of the Architecture School. Bob and Larry inspired the project throughout. Without their support, criticism, suggestions and guidance, we could not have done it at all.

PHOTO ACKNOWLEDGMENTS

Many of the pictures we have selected for this book come from secondary and tertiary sources. In every case we have tried to locate the original photographer and make the appropriate acknowledgment. In some cases, however, the sources are too obscure, and we have simply been unable to track them down. In these cases, we regret that our acknowledgments are incomplete and hope that we have not offended anyone.